THINKING YOUR WAY THROUGH ENGLISH GRAMMAR

EDMUND VITALE, JR.

H&H PUBLISHING COMPANY
1231 KAPP DR.
CLEARWATER, FLORIDA 34625

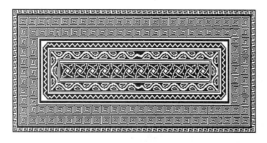

THINKING YOUR WAY THROUGH ENGLISH GRAMMAR

by
Edmund Vitale, Jr.
Gaithersburg, Maryland
Copyright 1992 Edmund Vitale, Jr.

H&H Publishing Company, Inc.
1231 Kapp Drive
Clearwater, Florida 34625
telephone (813) 442-7760

Editorial/Production Supervision
Robert Hackworth

Editor
Karen H. Davis

Cover Design
Tom Howland

Production Assistants
Mike Ealy, Sally Marston

ISBN 0-943202-36-1

Library of Congress Card Catalog Number 91-075142

Printing is the lowest number: 10 9 8 7 6 5 4 3 2

Perhaps . . . we shall embark upon a . . . revolution in language instruction. This will be a radical departure from present practices, which stress the communicative and artistic uses of words, to the neglect of the problem-solving function. Students are taught grammar, composition, creative writing and English literature — subjects which (as conventionally taught) have little to do with the logical process of thought. Seldom are students given formal, rigorous training in definition, classification, and other problem solving functions.

          *   *   *

Perhaps all of us, by learning to use words more skillfully, can elevate our analytical ability and transform our view of the world.

From: Richard W. Samson, <u>Thinking Skills: A guide to logic and comprehension</u>, Innovative Sciences, Inc. Cary, NC, 1988, p.79. Reprinted by permission of the publisher.

PREFACE

This book is a unique learning experience for teacher and student alike. Two overriding themes helped shape the nature of this unusual text.

THE THEORY

One — thinking and problem solving skills are used to teach English grammar content. These higher order skills are not taught separately or occasionally; they form the integral teaching methodology by which English grammar is taught throughout the book. Once thinking and problem solving skills become the basis by which content is taught, what happens in the classroom changes. A major change is away from an emphasis on rule memorization, right/wrong answers, and exercise sheets to an in-depth, open-ended exploration and construction of grammar knowledge and concepts by learners. Another change that occurs is that cognitive skill mastery is valued as highly as content mastery.

Two — learners are actively engaged in the learning process. Instead of being material directed, this text is learner directed. That is, the book attempts to take learners where they are, not where they should be according to grade level or course description, and from that point, requires them to actively participate in the construction of their own learning. (The research, analysis, discussion, and strategy development activities posed by this text are described below.) This learner-directed emphasis also changes significantly what happens in the classroom. Now the goal is not to cover a prescribed amount of material but to facilitate and guide the learners to build an understanding of the subject matter in a deeper and more significant way through problem-solving techniques.

THE THEORY INTO PRACTICE

These two overriding educational themes have been put into application in this book in a number of ways. The first strikingly different aspect of this book is that it contains a long series of questions built around various grammatical themes. To answer these questions, the learners must explore their English handbook, English grammar text, and/or dictionary. Any advanced English grammar text or handbook will do. (I've even taught this course very successfully with each learner having a different handbook!)

There are a great many transferable life-long learning skills encouraged by assigning questions and problems for solutions rather than assigning pages: learners are actively engaged in their learning, they develop good research and reference skills, they come to value their text as a source of answers that can be used after the class is over, they are encouraged to support answers with reasons, etc.

A second thinking technique used to bring the two major educational themes into application is to have each learner pose questions and come up with acitivities for him or her to teach the rest of the class. "Think Like A Teacher" activities are based on the premise that instructors learn best when preparing to teach so why not have learners learn in that manner also. These active learning exercises are met with apprehension at first but soon become so popular that learners can't wait to teach their classmates what they have learned.

A third important application of these theories is the activities that require learners to relate the steps their minds took to come up with answers to questions. This cognitive awareness becomes the basis for developing in learners an analytical and strategic approach to problem solving.

A fourth critical aspect of the teaching methodology that the thinking skills and active learning themes produce is that learners are encouraged to find relationships among a wide variety of terms and ideas. The openness of this approach promotes knowledge as something learners can construct for themselves, not as something to be slavishly memorized for the next test and soon forgotten. Much knowledge is ambiguous and is certainly ambiguous in application. By teaching to the ambiguity of knowledge, this book encourages learners to view knowledge as a basis for thinking; to value the necessity of supporting their point of view, not just search for the "right" answer; and to be tolerant of different points of view.

There are other skills promoted by this text: oral communication skills are developed in the numerous class discussions, self-confidence is promoted when reasons for answers are valued as much as answers themselves, learning how to learn — the most valued skill in the rapidly changing workplace — is explicitly encouraged.

The layout of the book is specifically designed to further the application of the two overriding themes by making learners aware of the thinking and problem solving skills being used to teach content. Boxes enclose themes, concepts, ideas, and thinking activities at appropriate points in the text. The specific thinking skill being used in a question is highlighted in the margin next to that section. The answer spaces and wide margins provide learners with plenty of room to answer questions and question answers, which helps reinforce the concept that the learners are responsible for actively constructing their own knowledge. The visual nature of many of the activities allows learners to actually see the relationships among the grammatical terms and concepts investigated in the text (especially how the part of speech of a word is determined by the function the word performs in a sentence), instead of only abstractly talking about these ideas.

Last but not least, this approach leads learners to a new appreciation and deeper understanding of English grammar. English grammar is viewed as an organized field of study capable of being analyzed for its own sake and also capable of being analyzed for solutions to grammatical problems in the learners' own writing. This text encourages learners to become self-motivated grammatical problem finders and then gives them the reference and research tools to become self-motivated problem solvers. They become problem solvers not because they have memorized rules and exceptions, but because they have been prompted to search, develop arguments, find support, and discuss various strategies, approaches, and answers.

The book also comes with a Teacher's Guide that gives very specific classroom techniques, together with suggested strategies, and a sampling of possible answers for the questions in this text. It is a complete guide to a constructive, active, learner-dominated classroom that uses thinking skills to teach content.

ACKNOWLEDGEMENTS

Many people, ideas, and books influence an author, most of which are not consciously appreciated, recognized, or even understood. I can still remember the first thinking skills conference I attended ("The National Conference on Teaching Thinking: The Cornerstone of Effective Education" in 1986 at Hilton Head, South Carolina) and knew intuitively that I had been exposed to something very profound. Being given the opportunity to teach English grammar and also to develop a thinking skills course at Spartanburg Technical College (South Carolina) had much to do with the development of the ideas that eventually produced this book. Richard Samson's Thinking Skills reinforced the connection between thinking, word meaning, thought, and grammar analysis.

I am forever indebted to Joan Slemenda, whose insight and creativity helped shape many of the innovative activities found in this book. Besides being a good listener as I struggled through the educational paradigm shift required to apply the idea of using thinking skills to teach content, she was particularly responsible for encouraging me to make the ideas and concepts as visual as possible.

To all the students in the English classes I taught using these methods, a hearty thank you. I particularly remember fondly the first class who experienced the earliest stages of the development of these methodologies and who still reacted positively (I thought almost enthusiastically given the subject matter!) to this "new" way of learning.

Carol Harrison, an English Instructor for Deaf Students at Spartanburg Technical College, has taught with this text for more than a year. She has inspired me not only with the classroom results she obtained but also with her suggestions and critiques for improving the text.

Jane Nickerson, Head of the English Department, and Cathy Baechle from the Center for Diagnostic Services of Gallaudet University School of Preparatory Studies, took the time and effort to read an early version of manuscript. Their comments and insights have been instrumental not only in the text itself but especially in the accompanying Teacher's Guide.

H&H Publishing in general, and editor Karen Davis in particular, have been patient, supportive, and excellent problem solvers as this text moved from manuscript to published form.

Finally, I want to thank my wife, Judie, and my daughters, Lisa and Tara, and my mother, Mary Vitale, for their encouragement and understanding during this long process.

In spite of the sincere and unselfish efforts of family, friends and colleagues, the finished product remains my responsibility, representing my dream as to how a course of study can be changed from a passive to a constructively active learning experience.

Ed Vitale
Gaithersburg, Maryland 1991

TABLE OF CONTENTS

WHY ENGLISH GRAMMAR?

A major goal of this book is for you to learn and have respect for the English language. English grammar, as a part of effective communication and writing, is one of the three courses (reading and math being the other two) that determines one's basic literacy in this country. Language, however, is even more important than that. It is the basic of the basics; one has to use language to think, to describe all the other subjects, including reading and math, and to problem solve.

We who speak English in the home have grown up with it as part of our development. Many of us, however, have not learned standard English. This nonstandard English is fine within a group that has agreed on meanings of particular words and phrases and sentence construction. But to communicate outside your group means you have to understand the new group's form of nonstandard English, or they have to learn yours. When you think of all the different groups that have their own way of phrasing ideas and their own meanings they give to words, you can see that it is an impossible task to learn all the different nonstandard languages. That's where standard, formal, written English comes into play. We have to communicate beyond our individual groups.

This problem is not limited to street language. Various professions and business areas also have their own way of communicating. Each profession not only has its own terms, it also has its own jargon, abbreviation system, and connotations for words. For everyone, standard, formal English is the common language through which we all communicate.

WHY THINKING?

Language also shapes our thinking process. It is the base upon which we reason, communicate, solve problems, and make decisions. This inti-

mate connection between language and thought is a major reason why thinking skills and activities are used in this book to help you understand English grammar.

Thinking involves *using* information not memorizing it. Memorization of rules and definitions (whether it is the rules of thinking skills or the rules of other courses) are not enough. Knowledge is growing rapidly and there is too much of it trying to get your attention. Our minds have limited space to retain all this knowledge. It is impossible to know everything about a particular subject or even a lot of things about several subjects. The important skills under these conditions are learning how to find, and then use, apply, and communicate information; not to memorize it. This is the thinking process.

A critical element in the thinking process is learning how to learn. This book emphasizes this important thinking skill by asking you many questions that require you to use your English handbook, text and / or dictionary as a reference source. The idea is to encourage you to learn how to use books to explore for answers. The more you explore, the more answers and explanations you can develop, the better thinker and problem solver you are.

Once learned in English grammar, learning to learn skills can be used in any course at school or in any training program in the workplace. Learning how to learn is the essential skill in the jobs you will get upon graduation. Technology is changing so rapidly that what you learn today will be replaced by new knowledge tomorrow. Business and industry are seeking employees who know how to learn and who can think for themselves: find information, analyze, question, evaluate, make decisions, and troubleshoot. Employers are not seeking those who have memorized the most rules or definitions. In other words, they want employees to USE the information, not just know about it.

Therefore learning how to learn and how to think are as important as learning English grammar as a fundamental skill. This book attempts to combine both.

ENGLISH GRAMMAR AND THE TAPESTRY OF THOUGHT AND COMMUNICATION

To solve problems effectively, the problem solver brings together a whole host of skills and knowlegdge. He or she must analyze the problem to be solved, brainstorm a wide variety of possible solutions, determine the goal he/she wants to achieve, evaluate the possible solutions by choosing the two or three that have the best potential to achieve the goal, and then test each of these two or three alternatives to determine which will best achieve the previously determined goal.

The foundation and basis for the problem-solving process are words and other symbols. Words are the medium not only for problem solving, but also for thought and communication, just as a warp and colored threads are the medium used by a weaver to create a tapestry. When the process of creating a tapestry begins, the weaver has a mental image of the design he wants to produce. He carefully analyzes alternatives and his medium and tools, integrating and manipulating these factors into his mental image of the final product. He then carefully selects the appropriate threads and weaves them into the framework of the warp; a design emerges, and he has thus expressed the image in his mind.

In like manner, a student creates a tapestry of communication when she attempts to express the thoughts in her mind. She thinks of what she wants to say, carefully selects the words, and places them within the framework of proper sentence structure. The student is analyzing her thoughts, manipulating the elements of grammar (parts of speech, word function, and sentence structure), and integrating them with her mental image of what she wants to disclose, to produce a well-developed communication. The thoughts in her mind are now expressed.

Thinking Your Way Through English Grammar concentrates on the English grammar component of the tapestry of written communication. It teaches the essence of English grammar holistically (instead of presenting grammar as a series of memorized rules) through "rigorous training in definition, classification, and other problem-solving functions." (Samson) Grammar rules are broadly explored as an organized field of study so that the student may then meaningfully relate them to the larger field of personal communication.

This text will allow the student to examine individual words in a sentence, seeing how versatile the language really is. The student will see that a part of speech is determined by how the word functions in a sentence. The student will also explore the relationships and comparisons of the elements, weaving them in various patterns, examining the ever-changing results.

Finally, the student will learn to appreciate the artistry of the careful selection and placement of individual words in the context of sentence structure to create a meaningful pattern of communication. This guide is unique because, in looking at the relationship of individual words to the whole and exploring grammar as an organized field of study, the student is forced to brainstorm, predict, evaluate, analyze, relate, make decisions, and think about her own thinking. She will learn valuable thinking skills that are transferable to learning content material in any other organized field of study.

Thinking Your Way Through English Grammar focuses attention holistically so that the student keeps the whole picture of grammar before her. Careful analysis is taught, but never for the sole purpose of learning individual elements only. The student will constantly be shifting her focus from analysis of rules to larger grammatical concepts, critical components of the imaginative and creative work of art called human communication.

TOPIC A:
INTEGRATING THE VOCABULARY OF GRAMMAR

The study of English grammar uses many terms. Just as a weaver carefully selects his threads and weaves them delicately and precisely, so must you understand the terms of English grammar and their relationships to one another.

Some of these terms may be familiar to you, like noun or verb. Other words, such as appositive or conjunctive adverb, may not be so familiar. Rather than learning isolated terms in the context of separate rules, you will have fun learning them through various thinking skill activities (labeling, categorizing, structured overviews, and classifying) that emphasize how the terms relate to one another. You see, the purpose of this section is not for you to memorize definitions but to understand the meaningful relationships of the terms of English grammar to each other.

Introduced here in Topic A is an underlying thread that goes through this entire text – being

aware of your own thinking. Instead of just answering a question, you focus on what your mind did to arrive at that answer. This is called metacognition. This thinking about thinking is like watching a time-elapsed film of the growth of a seed. As the seed sprouts and emerges from the ground, it struggles to grow, one step at a time. Although each step of this growth process may not be visible, it does take place.

In the same way, you may not be conscious of your thought process and think that answers just come into your brain. Your mind, however, does go through a series of steps — sometimes very quickly — to arrive at answers and to make decisions. As you go through this course, make a conscious effort to be aware of the steps your mind goes through as it answers questions and solves problems. Take a time-elapsed picture of your mind; be aware of how you process information.

BRAINSTORMING

A1. Your first activity is to list all of the names, terms, or labels you remember about English grammar. Don't pick and choose just the ones with which you are most familiar. Write all the grammatical terms you've ever seen or heard—including the ones you don't understand.

A2. Next, your instructor will conduct a brainstorming activity with the class. Each class member (including the instructor) must contribute at least one grammatical term without duplication. Use the space below to write additional words that you had not previously given in answer to A1.

GET BEYOND FRUSTRATION

A3. Now as a group, brainstorm for five more minutes. List all the additional words here.

A4. On the lines on the left below, place in alphabetical order all the grammatical terms the class has brainstormed. This is the first step in creating a personal glossary. To be able to use this glossary throughout the course, you have to know where to find the word you want to define. Therefore think about how the term *independent clause* should be alphabetized; should it go under "i," "c," or both? You have to make similar decisions with terms like *proper noun, personal pronoun*, etc.

There are three terms, important to the exercises in this study guide, that have been included in your personal glossary: *characteristic, function,* and *part of speech*. These terms have been defined since this study guide uses these words in special ways not found in most English texts.

A

_____

_____

_____

_____

_____

_____

B

_____

_____

C

_____

_____

_____

_____ In this study guide, characteristics refer to the distinguishing features of the part of
Characteristic speech of a word as used in a sentence. For example, a <u>noun</u> in a sentence can have
the characteristics of being either
  common or proper,
  singular or plural,
  concrete or abstract.

A <u>verb</u> has features, among others, such as
  helping or main,
  linking or action,
  past or present, etc.

A <u>pronoun</u> can be distinguished by person, case (personal, indefinite, relative),
singular or plural, to name a few.

_____

_____

C, continued

_____

_____

_____

_____

D

_____

_____

_____

E

_____

_____

F

————————————

————————————

————————————

Function ———————————— As used in this study guide, function refers to how words are used in a sentence, what purpose the word(s) performs in the dynamics of the sentence. For instance, nouns and pronouns perform (function) as:
> subject,
> object of a preposition,
> direct object, etc.

Other function terms include predicate, appositive, clause, simple sentence, to name only a few. See also *Part of Speech*.

G

————————————

————————————

H

————————————

I

————————————

I, continued

_____

J

_____

K

_____

L

_____

_____

M

_____

_____

_____

N

_____

_____

_____

_____

_____

_____

O

_____

_____

P

_____

Parts of Speech   The eight categories into which each word of the English language can be placed: nouns, pronouns, adjectives, verbs, adverbs, prepositions, conjunctions, and interjections. Some part of speech terms are also <u>function</u> terms:

>adjective,
>adverb,
>preposition,
>conjunction.

Noun, pronoun, and verb are strictly part of speech terms and not function terms. See also *Function*.

P, continued

_____

_____

_____

_____

_____

_____

_____

Q

_____

Q, continued

_____

_____

R

_____

_____

_____

S

_____

_____

_____

S, continued

_____

_____

_____

_____

_____

T

_____

_____

_____

_____

T, continued

_____

_____

_____

U

_____

V

_____

_____

_____

W

_____

XYZ

_____

A5. Now go back over your alphabetized list of grammatical terms and put the word "Know" in front of all the words you think you can define without looking them up in the textbook or dictionary. Then write your own definition (without looking it up) to the right of the word. (Leave some space for a more formal definition which will be required later.)

DID YOU REALLY KNOW THE DEFINITION?

EVALUATING

A6. These next questions are very important.
Did you <u>really</u> know the definitions of those terms?

What difficulty did you experience in trying to write the definition of a term that you thought you knew?

Did you find yourself at a loss for words? Why?

If remembering the definitions was not difficult, why was it easy for you?

A7. Is it important to define grammatical terms? Why?

Does defining English grammatical terms always lead to an <u>understanding</u> of the English language? Why?

DISCUSSING

A8. Discuss these questions in depth with the class. Note here any insights that you want to remember from the class discussion.

DEMAND ACCURACY - USE THE TEXTBOOK

A9.   Now write the textbook or dictionary definition of the words you had marked "Know" below <u>your</u> definition in A4.

HOW ACCURATE WERE YOU?

A10. Compare your definitions with the textbook's definitions. What observations can you make about the two sets of definitions?

COMPARING

A11. Discuss with the class the differences between your definition and the textbook's; which is more useful and why. Note here any insights or particularly interesting observations raised during the class discussion.

DISCUSSING

PROCESS: ANALYZE HOW YOU REMEMBER INFORMATION

A12. How can you remember precise definitions?

REMEMBERING

A13. Is it enough just to memorize information?

A14. Discuss as a class your answers to A12 and A13. Concentrate on how you go about remembering. Brainstorm as many different ways to recall information as you can. Note any points that you want to remember from the class discussion.

DEMAND ACCURACY - USE RESOURCES

A15. Complete your glossary by writing the textbook or dictionary definition of the terms not yet defined.

In this study guide, you will learn that every word in a sentence can be looked at in three different ways: its part of speech, or its characteristics, or its function. For instance, in the sentence, "The cat is furry," the word cat is a noun from a part of speech point of view, is a subject from a function point of view, and is singular, concrete, and common from the characteristics point of view. These three grammatical terms and their interrelationships are an important analytical thread running through the rest of this study guide.

FIND RELATIONSHIPS - LABELING

A16. Labeling is an exercise that you can use to help you learn. The exercise on the following page presents groups of two to three words. Your task is to determine what the words have in common and write a word or phrase that best describes the category on the line above. In the following example,

> a
> an
> the

you might label them either as adjectives (which is a general categorization) or as articles (which is the more specific).

A. _____
   future
   past
   present

B. _____
   main
   helping
   action

C. _____
   personal
   possessive
   indefinite

D. _____
   1st person
   singular
   objective

E. _____
   singular
   common
   concrete

F. _____
   plural
   proper
   abstract

G. _____
   subject
   predicate nominative

H. _____
   simple
   compound
   complete

I. _____
   simple
   compound
   complex

J. _____
   object of preposition
   direct object
   indirect object

K. _____
   dependent
   subordinate

L. _____
   independent
   main
   principal

M. _____
   while
   when
   since

N. _____
   but
   or
   so

O. _____
   gave
   hit
   threw

P. _____
   am
   is
   are

Q. _____
   very
   too
   quite

R. _____
   by
   toward
   under

S. _____
   course
   walk
   love

T. _____
   well
   quickly
   beautifully

U. _____
   good
   quick
   beautiful

V. _____
   everyone
   anyone
   everybody

W. _____
   to the race
   to the dance
   to the play

X. _____
   to race
   to dance
   to play

```
┌─────────────────────────────┐
│   PROCESS: ANALYZE HOW YOU   │
│      SOLVED THE PROBLEM      │
└─────────────────────────────┘
```

BEING AWARE

A17. What did your mind have to do to solve these labeling problems? Write your step-by-step procedure here.

STEP ONE:

STEP TWO:

STEP THREE:

STEP FOUR:

Discuss your procedure with the rest of the class and note here any interesting points you want to remember.

```
┌─────────────────────────────┐
│     THINK LIKE A TEACHER     │
└─────────────────────────────┘
```

CREATING

A18. Now it is your turn to create similar problems. Prepare three exercises, on separate paper, like the word groups in A16. Your instructor will choose one of your problems for you to place on the chalk board (without answers) and ask you to lead a class discussion on its solution.

Note here points that you want to remember.

A19. You have completed some labeling exercises using grammatical terms. How does this kind of exercise help in remembering the meanings of these words?

EVALUATING

A20. Note here any points you want to remember from the class discussion of A19.

┌─────────────────────────────────────┐
│ ANALYZE A SENTENCE: PARTS OF   │
│   SPEECH AND CHARACTERISTICS   │
└─────────────────────────────────────┘

A21. Below is a sentence on which you will practice finding relationships between parts of speech of a word used in a sentence and the characteristics of that word. Refer to the definitions of these terms in the glossary and the comments in A15. Write the part of speech of each word in the blank box above the word and the characteristics of the part of speech the word represents above that. Here is an example:

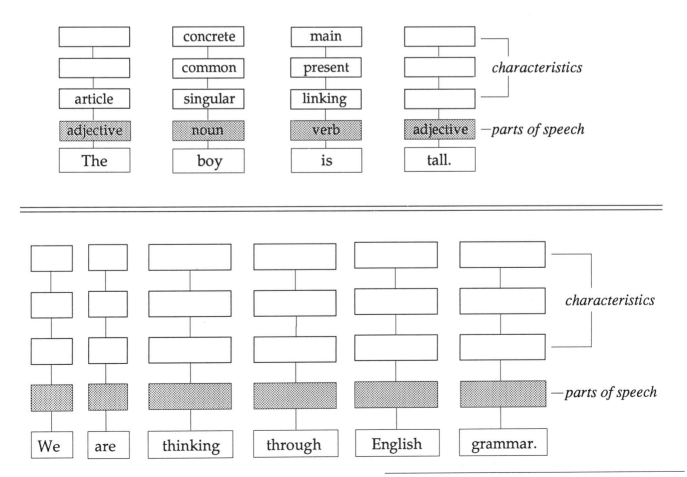

A22. This exercise in categorization has groups of three or four words, one of which does not relate to the others. Your task is to determine which word does not fit, cross it out, and state the reason for your decision. For example,

    house
    car
    red
    garage
    REASON: I will cross out red because it's an adjective and the remaining three words are nouns.

A. tense
   abstract
   concrete
   proper
   REASON:

B. predicate
     nominative
   subject
   direct object
   verb
   REASON:

C. mood
   common
   irregular
   helping
   REASON:

D. singular
   plural
   adjective
   possessive
   REASON:

E. gerund
   conjunction
   participle
   infinitive
   REASON:

F. preposition
   verbal
   interjection
   conjunction
   REASON:

G. verb
   complete
      predicate
   subject/verb
      agreement
   compound
      predicate

REASON:

H. person
   singular
   common
   objective

REASON:

I. at
   against
   off
   during

REASON:

J. badly
   sadly
   friendly
   gladly

REASON:

K. love
   hope
   delight
   pavement

REASON:

L. I
   he
   them
   she

REASON:

M. predicate
      nominative
   direct object
   object of
      preposition
   indirect object

REASON:

N. complex
   compound
   subordinate
   simple

REASON:

```
┌─────────────────────────────┐
│  PROCESS: ANALYZE HOW YOU   │
│    SOLVED THE PROBLEM       │
└─────────────────────────────┘
```

BEING AWARE

A23. What did your mind have to do to solve these categorization problems? Write your step-by-step procedure here.

STEP ONE:

STEP TWO:

STEP THREE:

STEP FOUR:

DISCUSSING

Discuss your procedure with the rest of the class and note here any interesting points you want to remember.

```
┌─────────────────────────────┐
│    THINK LIKE A TEACHER     │
└─────────────────────────────┘
```

CREATING

A24. Now it is your turn to create similar problem categories. Develop five exercises, on separate paper, like the word groups in A22. Your instructor will choose one of your problems for you to place on the chalk board (without answers) and ask you to lead a class discussion on its solution. Note here any points that you want to remember.

> PROCESS: CATEGORIZE TO
> REMEMBER INFORMATION

A25. You have completed some categorizations of grammatical terms. How does this kind of exercise help in remembering the meanings of these words?

EVALUATING

A26. Discuss your answer to A25 with the class. Note here any insights that you want to remember from the class discussion.

DISCUSSING

> ANALYZE A SENTENCE: PARTS OF SPEECH,
> CHARACTERISTICS, AND FUNCTIONS

A27. Below is the same sentence you initially saw in A21. Fill in the parts of speech and characteristics that you used in A21. This time you will add the function terms. Please review the definition of function as set forth in your glossary. Then fill in the boxes below the sentence that indicate how the word(s) are <u>used</u>, the *function* of the word(s), in the sentence. As you do this exercise, begin to look for relationships among the these terms, i.e., what are the characteristics of nouns and what are the functions nouns can perform in a sentence, etc.

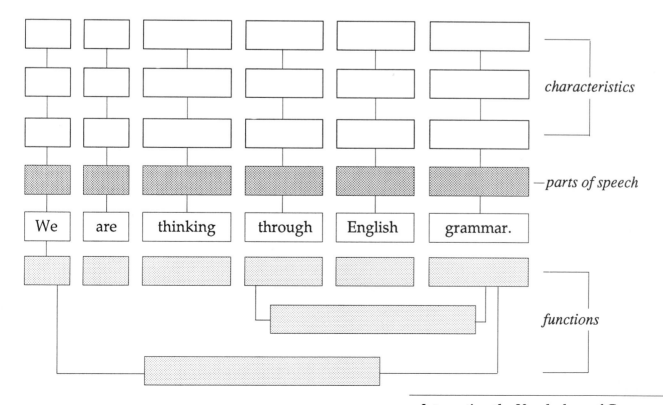

We | are | thinking | through | English | grammar.

characteristics

—parts of speech

functions

A28. The structured overview is another technique to force you to <u>use</u> the meanings of words and to determine <u>relationships</u> among them. It presents a graphically visual picture of how ideas and/or words relate to each other. If, for example, you were given the four words *of, preposition, on,* and *over,* and were asked to place them in the following chart,

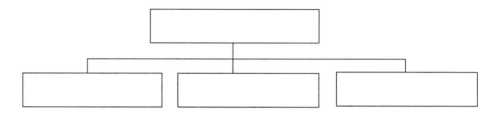

you would put the word *preposition* in the top box since it is the label of the major category. The other words are examples of prepositions and would be placed in the boxes below in no particular order.

In the following exercises, use the given words to fill in the appropriate boxes to show the best relationship among the words. Explain the reasons for your choice in the space provided.

A.

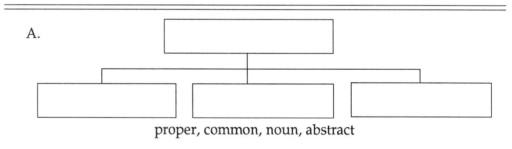

proper, common, noun, abstract

REASON:

B.

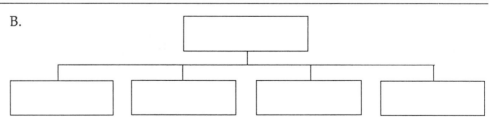

direct object, indirect object, noun,
predicate nominative, object of preposition

REASON:

C.

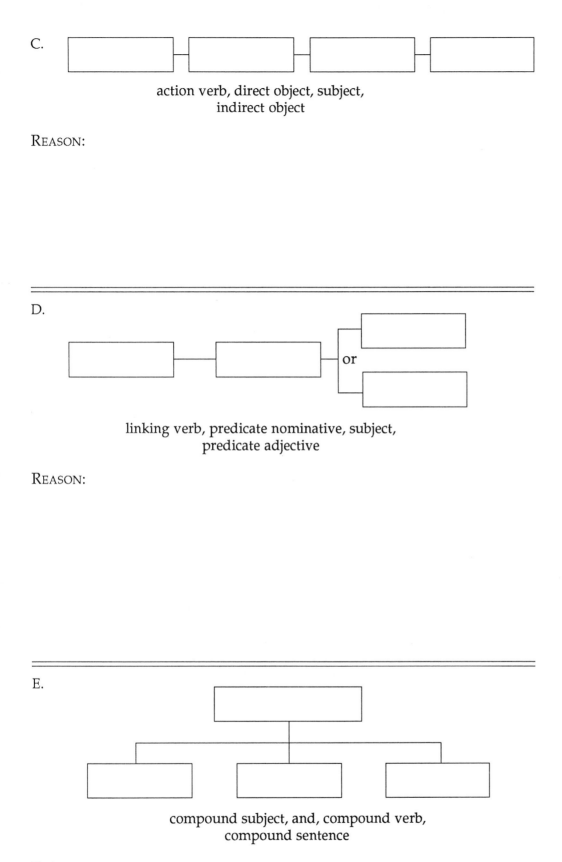

action verb, direct object, subject,
indirect object

REASON:

D.

linking verb, predicate nominative, subject,
predicate adjective

REASON:

E.

compound subject, and, compound verb,
compound sentence

REASON:

F.

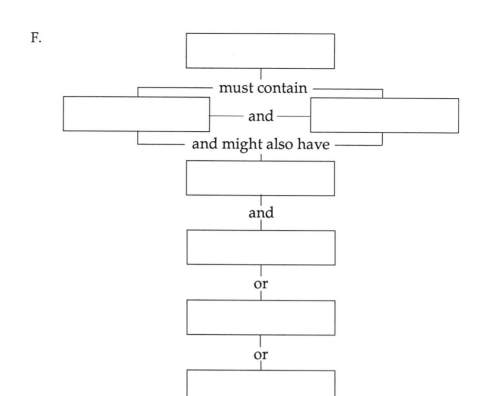

must contain

and

and might also have

and

or

or

direct object, subject, indirect object, verb,
predicate nominative, predicate adjective, sentence

REASON:

G.

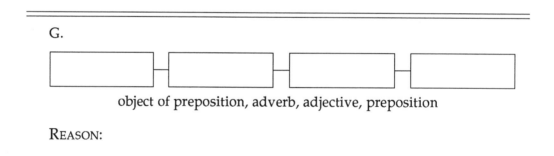

object of preposition, adverb, adjective, preposition

REASON:

H.

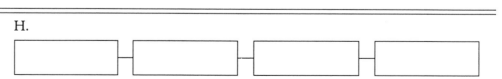

double quotation mark, double quotation mark,
single quotation mark, single quotation mark

REASON:

I.

	is the		of	

	is the		of	

contraction, whose, who, possessive, who's, who is

REASON:

J.

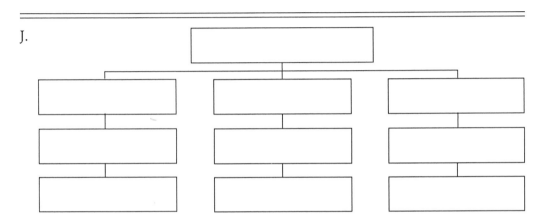

adjective, gerund, dancing, tired, noun,
noun, infinitive, verbal, to run, participle

REASON:

K.

	=		+	

	=		+	

	=		+	

independent clause, verb, dependent clause,
simple sentence, independent clause, compound
sentence, subject, independent clause, complex sentence

REASON:

L.

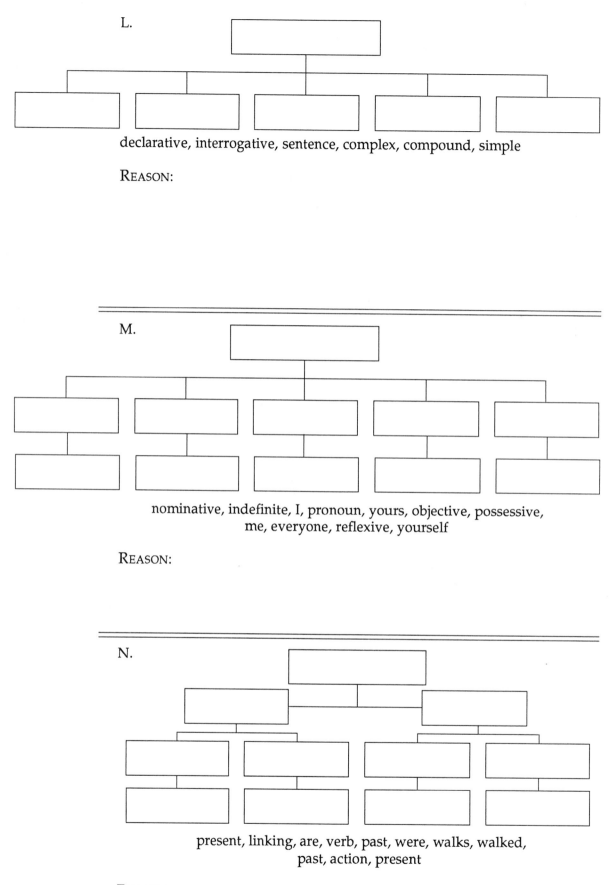

declarative, interrogative, sentence, complex, compound, simple

REASON:

M.

nominative, indefinite, I, pronoun, yours, objective, possessive,
me, everyone, reflexive, yourself

REASON:

N.

present, linking, are, verb, past, were, walks, walked,
past, action, present

REASON:

A29. What did your mind have to do to solve these structured overview problems? Write your step-by-step procedure here.

BEING AWARE

STEP ONE:

STEP TWO:

STEP THREE:

STEP FOUR:

Discuss your procedure with the rest of the class and note here any interesting points you want to remember.

CREATING

A30. Now it's your turn to create some partial structured overviews. Using the grammar terms provided, draw boxes to represent the proper relationships among the words. IDEA! You may want get some index cards (or cut up some paper), write the words on them, and actually manipulate the terms until you get a right relationship. Then draw your structured overview in the space provided.

A.

gerund, verbal, infinitive, participle

B.

adverb, adjective, adverb, verb

C.

dependent clause, verb, subject, subordinating conjunction

D.

who, because, subordinating conjunction, dependent word signals,
relative pronouns,while, which

┌─────────────────────────────────────┐
│ THINK LIKE A TEACHER, AGAIN!   │
└─────────────────────────────────────┘

A31. Now it is your turn to create five complete structured overviews on
separate paper. Your instructor will choose one of your problems for you
to place on the board (blank boxes with words underneath) and ask you to
lead a class discussion on its solution. Note here any important points made
during the discussion.

CREATING

┌─────────────────────────────────────┐
│ PROCESS: USE STRUCTURED OVERVIEWS   │
│   TO REMEMBER INFORMATION   │
└─────────────────────────────────────┘

A32. You have completed some structured overview exercises using
grammatical terms. How does this kind of exercise help in remembering the
meanings of these words?

EVALUATING

A33. Discuss your answer to A32 with the class. Note here any insights that
you want to remember from the class discussion.

DISCUSSING

A34. Fill in the parts of speech, characteristics, and functions for each word in the sentence below. Be aware of how part of speech and function interact with each other.

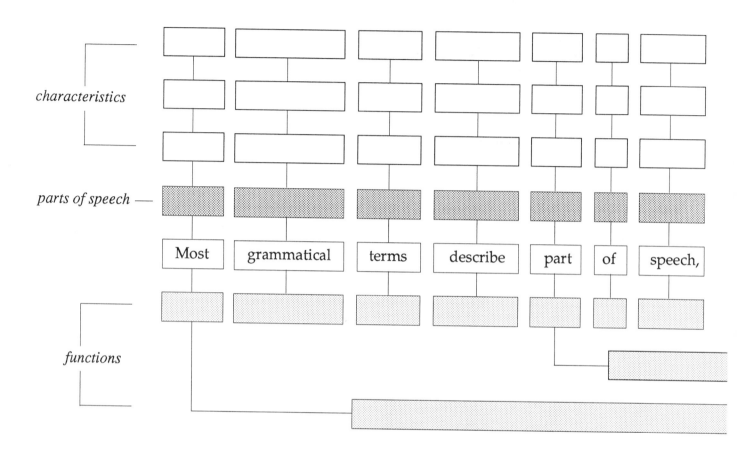

characteristics

parts of speech —

Most | grammatical | terms | describe | part | of | speech,

functions

LOOK FOR RELATIONSHIPS - CLASSIFICATION

CLASSIFYING

A35. Classification is a process in which you systematically group items into categories according to similar characteristics. It is a thinking skill that enables you to discover what relationships exist among items. The alphabetizing of words (as you did with grammatical terms in A4) is a classification system: grouping words together according to similar first letters. (The major purpose of this classification system is to organize grammatical terms alphabetically, and the letters of the alphabet constitute the subclassification system.)

Now that you have precise definitions of grammatical terms in A4 and some experience in categorizing and labeling, classify all the words you have listed in A4 under one of the five headings listed at the right. (The purpose here might be called: Major Grammatical Term Groups.) Be prepared to give your reasons for putting each word in the category that you did.

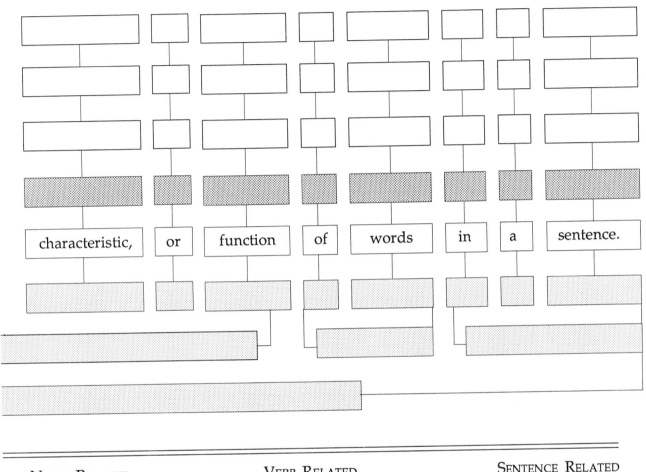

characteristic, or function of words in a sentence.

NOUN RELATED   VERB RELATED   SENTENCE RELATED

PUNCTUATION RELATED   GRAMMATICAL ERRORS RELATED

BEING AWARE

A36. What did your mind have to do to solve this classification problem? Write your step-by-step procedure here.

STEP ONE:

STEP TWO:

STEP THREE:

STEP FOUR:

DISCUSSING

Discuss your procedure to solve this classification problem with the rest of the class and note here any interesting points you want to remember.

THINK LIKE A TEACHER

LABELING

A37. Now it is your turn to make up a classification system. Develop a major purpose and then determine a subclassification system with at least 3 labels consistent with each other and consistent with the major purpose. Place the words from your glossary into your classification system and put a label on each group. (You can't use the same classification system used in the previous question.)

MAJOR PURPOSE:

LABEL:

LABEL:

LABEL:

LABEL:

A38. Below and on the following page is a classification chart that has the major purpose and categories already labeled. Your task is to place the grammatical terms you listed in A4 together with the additional grammatical terms found in A16, A22, and A28 in the appropriate categories.

MAJOR PURPOSE: The Three Categories into Which this Text Classifies Most Grammatical Terms

LABEL: Terms that Name Parts of Speech

LABEL: Terms that Describe Characteristics of Parts of Speech

Keep a separate list of the terms that don't fit in the other three categories here.

PROCESS: CLASSIFY TO REMEMBER INFORMATION

REMEMBERING

A39. You have completed some classification exercises using grammatical terms. How does this kind of exercise help in remembering the meanings of these words?

DISCUSSING

A40. Discuss your answer to A39 with the class. Note here any insights that you want to remember from the class discussion.

SYNTHESIZE: PUTTING IT ALL TOGETHER

SYNTHESIZING

A41. On a separate paper, create a chart that compares the difficulties and/or ease, benefits and/or detriments of the exercises of labeling, categorization, structured overview, and classification as they relate to remembering and properly using English grammatical terms.

A42. Do you think you have a good understanding of English grammar terms? Why or why not?

A43. Have you "learned to learn" in the context of English grammar? State your reasons for your answer giving specific details.

A44. Write a paragraph or two that explains how you can use the exercises of labeling, categorization, structured overview, and classification to help you learn and understand other subjects. Specifically, pick one of your other courses and give specific examples that show how the exercises presented here can help you learn that other subject.

A45. The last exercise in this topic is to analyze another sentence from the point of view of parts of speech, characteristics, and functions. Again, note carefully how these three ways of looking at words in a sentence interrelate with each other.

Don't hesitate to use your textbook and/or dictionary to help solve this one. Be prepared to defend your answers.

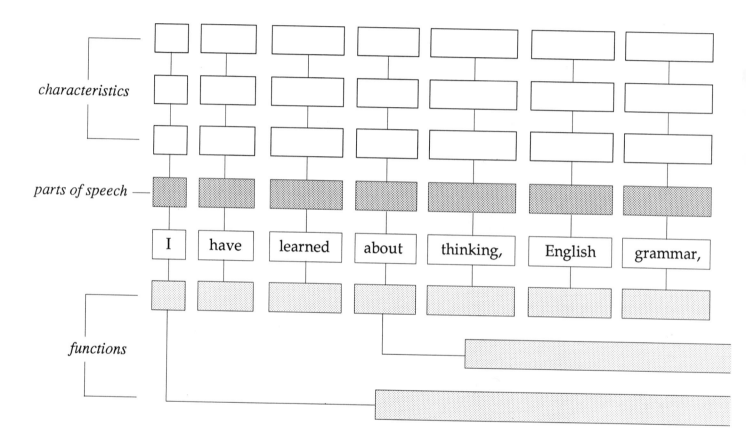

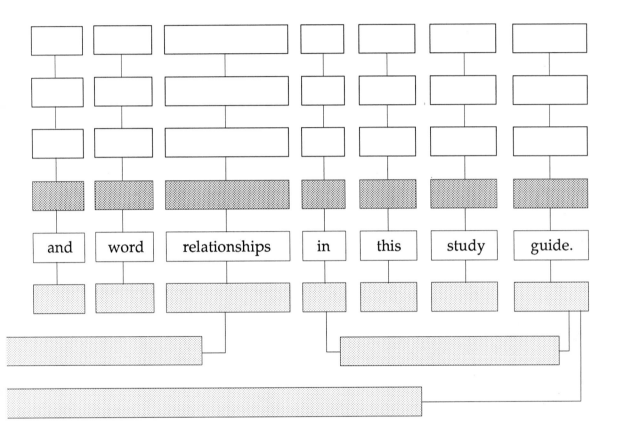

and   word   relationships   in   this   study   guide.

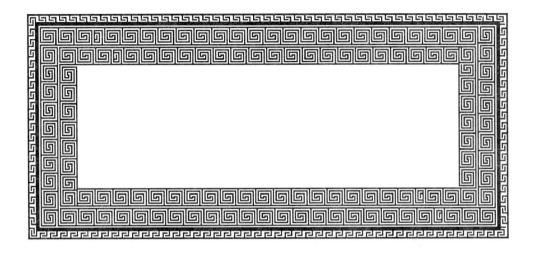

TOPIC B:
ANALYZING SUBJECT/VERB AGREEMENT

Now that you see how grammatical terms are interwoven and interrelated, you are going to analyze subject/verb agreement in the same manner. In going through this analysis, you will be adding richer, more meaningful knowledge to your tapestry of English.

Topic B will lead you through a four-step process of solving subject/verb agreement problems. You will learn all the English rules you need to know about each part of the process—no more, no less. This knowledge base of English rules is the foundation upon which this Topic will require you to think about and work with the wonderful diversity of the English language.

Here in Topic B is a second underlying thread– reference skills. You will not be assigned pages or chapters to read. Instead, you will be given questions that will send you searching through textbooks and dictionaries. These books, which you may have once considered to be dull and boring, now become interesting and informative. Because you are researching and analyzing information to solve a specific problem, learning will be more effective and your knowledge will last longer.

You will also be asked to provide proof for your answers. This is a further development of the skill of being aware of your thinking that was introduced in Topic A. This is an important thinking skill! Remember, it is as vital to show where and how you got your information as it is to give an answer.

FIND A STARTING POINT - MAKE
CONNECTIONS WITH REFERENCE SKILLS

SEARCHING

B1.   In your textbook, find the pages on which the topic *subject/verb agreement* is discussed. Write those page numbers here.

B2.   In which part of the textbook did you first look to answer B1?

Where else could you have looked?

B3.   In searching for information, it is sometimes a problem to know which part of the book to use. It is also sometimes difficult to determine (1) which word to focus on in an index or (2) how to use a table of contents to find information you want. The author of the book might not use the same words for the terms you are looking for.

QUESTIONING

What questions did you ask yourself to help you start your search to answer B1?

What were some words you could have looked for in the index to start your search to answer B1?

How do you go about finding this information from the Table of Contents in your book?

What's another way you might have found this information?

EVALUATING

B4.   Which method of finding information do you find useful and why?

Be prepared to discuss your answers in class. Note here any points you want to remember from the class discussion.

B5.   As a class, brainstorm <u>problems</u> you have in trying to find information in indexes, yellow pages, phone books, encyclopedias, reader's guides, etc. Note here any interesting points made during the class discussion.

BRAINSTORMING

Again, as a class, brainstorm possible strategies you could use to solve these problems. Note here any points of interest made during class discussion.

B6.   Find the definition of subject/verb agreement in the section in your textbook that discusses subject/verb agreement. Write the text's definition for subject/verb agreement here.

SEARCHING

On which page is this definition found?

B7.   Does your textbook contain a section of definitions?
If yes, what is that section called?

B8.   If you have a special definitional section in your textbook, how is subject/verb agreement defined in this section?

DEFINING

On which page is this definition found?

QUESTIONING

B9.   As you think further about subject/verb agreement, formulate some questions that you could ask yourself about the topic. For example:

1. How are parts of speech related to subject/verb agreement?

Note your questions here:

QUESTION 1.

QUESTION 2.

QUESTION 3.

DISCUSSING

B10. Discuss with the class the questions that were written in B9. Use these questions as a framework for your learning subject/verb agreement. In working through this study guide, you will have an opportunity to answer these questions for yourself. Note here important points made during the class discussion.

> LET'S WRITE . . .

CREATING

B11. Write a 3 paragraph essay about "My Favorite T.V. Show." Please triple space the essay.

B12. You are about to start an investigation of a four step process to solve subject/verb agreement problems. Instead of just memorizing the steps, you will be asked to investigate (using your reference skills) the reasoning behind each step, including the definitions and relationships of terms, and then apply each step to exercises and the essay you have completed. (Each step of the process is introduced at appropriate places in the text.)

Be prepared to discuss any question you might have concerning this explanation.

FIND A STARTING POINT - MAKE
CONNECTIONS WITH REFERENCE SKILLS

B13. You discovered that the definition of subject/verb agreement requires the knowledge of the meanings of the terms used in the definition. The next few questions investigate some of these other definitions. What is the definition of *subject* as it appears in your textbook?

DEFINING

On which page is this definition found?

B14. In what part of the textbook did you look for that definition? Why?

B15. Can you tell from the definition of subject what part of speech the subject should be?

B16. Copy the definition of *noun* from your textbook.

DEFINING

On which page is this definition found?

B17. Copy the definition of *pronoun* from your textbook.

On which page is this definition found?

HOW THINGS RELATE - MAKE
CONNECTIONS THROUGH ANALYSIS

EXPLAINING

B18. Explain in your own words how the terms *subject*, *nouns*, and *pronouns* relate to each other.

HOW THINGS RELATE - A
VISUALIZATION TECHNIQUE

B19. Now, show in the structured overview below how subject, nouns, and pronouns relate to each other.

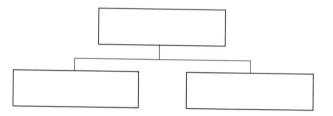

EVALUATING

B20. Which statement below, if either, is true? Explain your answer.

    a. All nouns and pronouns function as subjects.
    b. All subjects are either nouns or pronouns.

Explain.

B21. In order for you to answer the previous question, you had to realize that nouns and pronouns can be used to perform other functions in a sentence besides being subjects. In the structured overview below, fill in the other functions for which nouns can be used. This will give you a visual representation of how versatile these two parts of speech are.

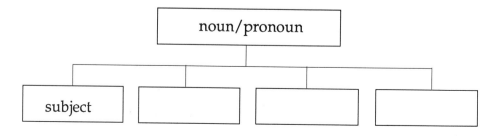

B22. You noticed in B21 that a noun and pronoun can be used either as an object of a preposition or as a subject. This distinction is crucial. For example, in the following sentence,

"The bridges over the river (is, are) extremely graceful,"

there are two nouns. Name them.

Can they both be the subject of the sentence?

Why?

B23. Do you see how you may be confused by which noun is the subject?   *DEFINING*

"Bridges" (noun) is the subject.
"River" (noun) is the object of the preposition.

The first step of the four-step subject/verb agreement process will help you avoid this possible confusion. These four steps will help you analyze your sentences to determine if the verb agrees with the subject in number. The first step starts this sentence analysis:

STEP ONE: CROSS OUT PREPOSITIONAL PHRASES.

To understand this step you will have to examine prepositions and prepositional phrases. (Don't forget it is the intention of this book to have you explore the reasons behind the rules!)

What is the definition of a preposition?

On which page is this definition found?

B24. Is this definition of a preposition useful? Why or why not?   *EVALUATING*

· ·
·   ·
·   ALERT!   TAKE A TIME-ELAPSED PICTURE   ·
·   OF YOUR MIND!   ·
·   ·
· ·

B25. List at least 10 prepositions.

B26. Did you recall these 10 words from memory or did you use the textbook?

Remember that you are trying to become aware of what your mind does so that for the following two questions, "I don't know" is not an acceptable answer. If you used the book, why did you pick those 10 words?

If you recalled from memory, how did <u>those</u> 10 words come into your mind?

REMEMBERING

B27. What is the easiest way for you to remember prepositions: by memorizing the definition or memorizing the prepositions themselves?

Explain your choice.

PRACTICE YOUR REFERENCE SKILLS

B28. Some prepositions can be other parts of speech. In which book can you look to determine the other part of speech a preposition might be?

List at least five prepositions that are also other parts of speech and name the part of speech.

DEFINING

B29. We are now going to use your knowledge of prepositions and your knowledge of objects of a preposition (discovered in the structured overview in B21) and relate them. Find the definitions of *phrase* and *prepositional phrase* in your textbook. Write each definition and the page number where found.

PHRASE

PREPOSITIONAL PHRASE

B30. How can you use the definition of the word *phrase* to explain why the object of a preposition cannot be the subject of a sentence?

B31. Compare the definition of prepositional phrase you found in your textbook to the following one:

> A prepositional phrase is a group of words that starts with a preposition and ends with a noun or pronoun (called the object of the preposition) and does not contain a subject or verb.

Note which of the two definitions is most useful to you and explain why.

EVALUATING

B32. Let's focus on the preposition *to*, which, in addition to being a preposition, is also associated with the infinitive. What is an infinitive?

Use the definitions of prepositional phrase and infinitive to explain how you know when *to* is functioning as a preposition and when it is functioning as part of an infinitive.

SYNTHESIZING

Can the infinitive be a part of speech?

If yes, what are the part(s) of speech?

If the infinitive can be a noun, can the infinitive function as the subject of a sentence?

What is your proof?

Write a sentence which uses the infinitive as a subject of the sentence.

CREATING

B33. You have discovered how to determine when *to* is used as a preposition and when it introduces an infinitive. In exercise B28, you noted prepositions that were other parts of speech. Using the definition of preposition and prepositional phrase, explain how you know when a word is being used as a preposition and when it is used as another part of speech.

SYNTHESIZNG

B34. Let's add to the structured overview started in B19. Using abbreviations, where would you put the grammatical terms *preposition, prepositional phrase, object of a preposition, noun,* and *pronoun* on the structured overview below? Also add 8 examples of prepositions, at least two of which also function as another part of speech, in the appropriate boxes. Finally, put asterisks (*) in the boxes of those prepositions that can be used as other parts of speech.

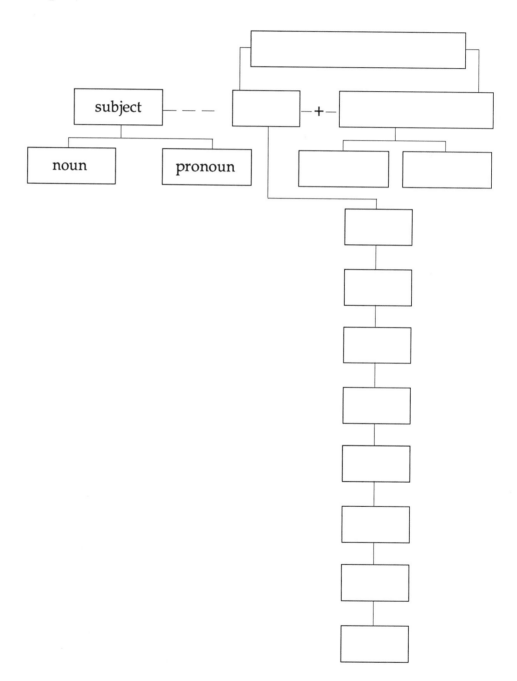

Be prepared to defend, in a class discussion, your placement of each term on the structured overview.

B35. The next step in the subject/verb agreement process is:

STEP TWO: CIRCLE THE SUBJECT

What method do you use to find subjects of a sentence?

EXPERIENCE / PRACTICE

APPLYING

B36. In the following practice sentences, (1) cross out prepositional phrases and (2) circle the subject. Be prepared to defend your work. Do not choose the verb at this time; you will do that later.

A. The bridges over the river [are, is] extremely graceful.

B. The long, narrow bridges over the rough, dirty river [are, is] extremely graceful.

C. Over the river and through the woods, to grandmother's house we [go, goes].

D. The winner in the local competition [go, goes] to the state fair finals.

E. John, of all people, [are, is] going to the doctor.

F. The scientific revolution of the last 20 to 30 years [has, have] sparked an interest in science and math.

G. Frank [are, is] driving to the park through many small towns and villages.

H. In addition to your financial argument, your points about the environmental impact [are, is] well taken.

I. [Are, Is] John driving to New York?

J. Jack [walk, walks] to the store.

K. The cat [were, was] hiding in the corner, for she was frightened by the storm.

L. To eat now [are, is] more convenient for me.

DISCUSSING

As a class, check and discuss the above practice sentences. Note here any problems you encountered and any insights you gained in the class discussion.

. . . AND CHECK IT OUT! . . .

PROOFREADING

B37. Using the essay you have written in B11, cross out the prepositional phrases and circle the subjects in each sentence. Hand in your essay to your instructor who will circle two sentences. Be prepared to place these two sentences on the board (without cross outs and circlings) and ask the class to cross out the prepositional phrases and circle the subjects, giving reasons for their choices.

B38. As we learned earlier, subjects don't always have to be nouns. Let's look at an example.

He, of all the boys, [are, is] on the football team.

(1)   Cross out the prepositional phrase and

(2)   Circle the subject.

What part of speech is the subject of that sentence?

How do you know?

List the personal pronouns, like *he*, that can be used as the subject of a sentence.

BEING AWARE

B39. How did you go about looking for this list of pronouns? Write all the steps, even the nonproductive ones, that you took to find these words.

STEP ONE:

STEP TWO:

STEP THREE:

STEP FOUR:

What does your textbook call these kinds of pronouns?

CLASSIFYING

On which page was this information found?

B40. Ask your teacher for another textbook. Find what that textbook calls *pronouns as subjects of a sentence.*

Write the name of the textbook and page number where you found this information.

B41. Discuss as a class the different names that were found for *personal pronouns as subjects of a sentence.* So many names for the same idea! Does that create a problem for you? Note here points of interest from the class discussion.

DISCUSSING

B42. Now go back to your original text. You have already noted that pronouns can be used as objects of prepositions (see B21, B34). But can the <u>same</u> personal pronouns you listed in B38 be used as the object of a preposition? _____ If not, list the form of the personal pronouns listed in B38 that can be used as an object of a preposition.

LISTING

How does the knowledge that personal pronouns change form when used for different functions help you to locate or use pronoun subjects?

B43. In your textbook, find the section that deals with *indefinite pronouns.* List the indefinite pronouns that can be used as subjects.

Page number where information is found.

B44. As with prepositions, indefinite pronouns can be used as other parts of speech. Below are two sentences that illustrate the differences.

> a. Each tree [are, is] tall.
> b. Each of the trees [are, is] tall.

Name the part of speech of the word *each* in sentence (a) above.

Name the part of speech of the word *each* in sentence (b) above.

ANALYZING

How can you tell when a word like *each* is acting as an indefinite pronoun or as an adjective?

LISTING

B45. List any other indefinite pronouns that could be used as another part of speech and list the part of speech for each.

What did you do to find the answer to this question?

DISCUSSING

B46. Discuss your answers to B42 through B45 with the rest of the class. Note here any important points made during the class discussion.

B47. Let's add to the structured overview started in B19 and further expanded in B34. First fill in the boxes already completed in B34. (Don't forget the asterisks!) Then place the abbreviations for the words *subjective pronoun*, *objective pronoun*, and *indefinite pronoun* in the appropriate boxes, together with examples of each. Put an asterisk (*) next to those examples that may function as another part of speech.

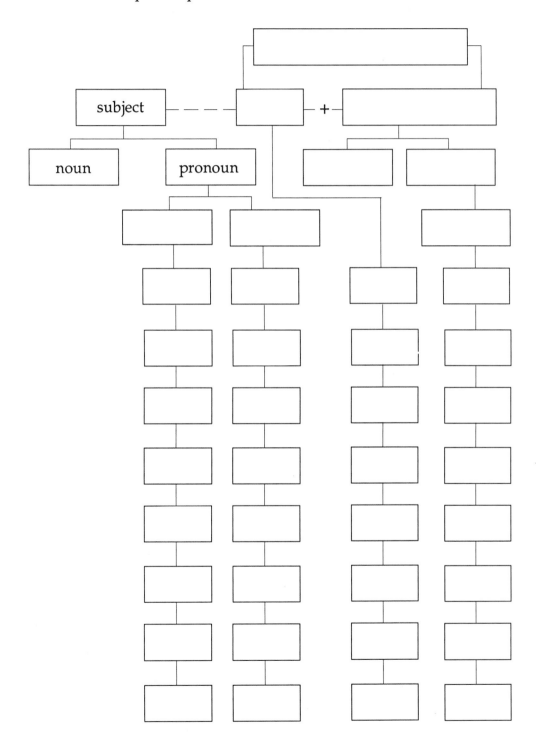

DISCUSSING

Be prepared to defend your placement of each of the terms in the structured overview in a class discussion. Note here any important points made during the class discussion.

```
THINK LIKE A TEACHER
```

CREATING

B48. Let's practice! Create 10 sentences that use nouns, personal pronouns, and indefinite pronouns as subjects. Include prepositional phrases in your sentences. Be prepared to write one or more of your sentences on the board and to be the teacher as your classmates perform the following steps:

1) Cross out prepositional phrases.
2) Circle the subject.
3) Determine whether the circled subject is a noun, pronoun, or indefinite pronoun, and the characteristics of the part of speech of the circled subject.

DISCUSSING

Note here any important points made during the class discussion.

```
ALERT! TAKE A TIME-ELAPSED PICTURE
OF YOUR MIND!
```

B49. In the following two sentences, cross out the prepositional phrase and circle the subject.

a) There [is, are] a kitten on the roof.
b) Here [is, are] the five kittens in the basket.

SEARCHING

B50. Find proof to determine whether *there* and *here* can be the subject of a sentence. Write the rule.

B51. How did you go about finding this information? List all the steps you took, including the ones that turned out to be wrong. How did you finally think of the approach that yielded the answer?

STEP ONE:

STEP TWO:

STEP THREE:

STEP FOUR:

B52. You are now ready for the third step in the subject/verb agreement process.

> STEP THREE: DETERMINE WHETHER THE SUBJECT IS SINGULAR OR PLURAL; PLACE IN THE MARGIN AN "S" IF THE SUBJECT IS SINGULAR OR "P" IF IT IS PLURAL.

This step requires you to analyze the subject for its singular or plural characteristics, a task you have done in Topic A. As you will soon find out, determining whether subjects are singular or plural has a great many special rules. Let's start with the first rule.

How are most nouns made plural? Write your text's answer here.

Page number where information is found.

B53. Most singular nouns add "s" or "es" to make them plural. If you need practice making this type noun plural, your instructor will assign pages in your textbook or give you worksheets so you may drill in this area. This is the first in a series of 18 rules that help determine whether a subject is singular or plural. These rules will be accumulated in B104. You will be instructed to write them there as you encounter the rule. This rule -- most singular nouns add "s" or "es" to make them plural -- will be referred to as Rule 1 and should be written in B104 opposite #1 now.

HOW DO YOU HANDLE EXCEPTIONS?

B54. Some nouns change their spelling to form the plural. List the singular and plural forms of 8 such nouns.

Formulate an appropriate rule to cover this situation. Be prepared to defend your wording, and, after a class consensus, write the rule here and in B104 as Rule 2.

B55. Some words are more difficult to classify as singular or plural. Use your textbook or dictionary to determine if the following words are singular or plural:

news_____ measles_____ mathematics_____

On which page is this information found?

Formulate an appropriate rule to cover this situation. Be prepared to defend your wording, and, after a class consensus, write the rule here and in B104 as Rule 3.

B56. *News* and *measles* look as if they should be plural but are not. Here are some words that represent one object. Are they singular or plural?

eyeglasses_____ scissors_____ pants_____ jeans_____

On which pages is this information found?

Formulate an appropriate rule to cover this situation. Be prepared to defend your wording, and, after a class consensus, write the rule here and in B104 as Rule 4.

B57. How are you going to remember these exceptions: nouns that change spelling to form the plural (B54), singular nouns that end in "s" (B55), and the words that represent one item but are considered plural (B56)?

Discuss your answer to this question with the class. Note here any important points made during the class discussion.

B58. Some texts label nouns referring to groups of people as collective nouns. Does your text use this term?

If not, what term does your text use for nouns such as *class*, *group* and *committee*?

On which page is this information found?

B59. Write the complete list of the *collective nouns* as they appear in your textbook.

B60. Write the textbook definition that determines when these nouns, acting as subjects, are singular and when they are plural.

B61. Write one sentence which uses *committee* as a singular subject and one which uses *committee* as a plural subject.

a)

b)

B62. Discuss the rule that covers this situation, any modifications of the rule you think should be made, and your two example sentences (B61) with the class. Note here any important points made during class discussion.

After the class discussion, write the rule the class has agreed upon here and in B104 as Rule 5.

B63. Here are two sentences in which the word *number* is the subject:

A. The number (is, are) large.
B. A number (is, are) going.

Try to determine, without using your text, in which sentence *number* is singular and in which it is plural.

B64. What is your textbook rule covering this situation and how does it compare to yours?

Formulate an appropriate rule to cover this situation. Be prepared to defend your wording, and, after a class consensus, write the rule here and in B104 as Rule 6.

> ### How Things Relate - Make Connections Through Analysis

QUESTIONING

B65. Are units of time (i.e. hours), weight (i.e. pounds), or money (i.e. dollars) considered singular or plural when used as a subject? For instance, here are three sentences:
   A. Five dollars [is, are] a lot of money.
   B. Three days [is, are] a long time.
   C. Fifty pounds [is, are] heavy.

PREDICTING

Each of these subjects is considered singular. Without reference to your text, try to devise a rule that would explain why these plural-looking subjects are singular.

FINDING PROOF

B66. Now use the textbook to answer B65 and write the textbook rule here.

On which page is this information found?

COMPARING

B67. Compare your rule with the textbook's rule and note similarities and differences.

Formulate a rule to cover this situation. Be prepared to defend your wording, and, after a class consensus, write the rule here and in B104 as Rule 7.

B68. Here are three sentences that use <u>titles</u> as subjects.

    A. <u>Walker, Jordan, and Post</u> [is, are] a law firm.
    B   <u>Creative Designs</u> [is, are] a designing company.
    C. <u>Great Expectations</u> [is, are] a good book.

Without looking in your textbook, try to determine whether these subjects are singular or plural and why.

PREDICTING

B69. Now, use your textbook to answer B68 and write the rule here.

FINDING PROOF

On which page is this information found?

B70. Compare your rule (B68) with that of the textbook's (B69).

COMPARING

Formulate a rule to cover this situation. Be prepared to defend your wording, and, after a class consensus, write the rule here and in B104 as Rule 8.

B71. How does trying to predict an answer to a question help you to remember the information you are looking up?

B72. Remember in B32 you discovered that an infinitive can act as a noun and therefore be the subject of a sentence. Is an infinitive acting as a subject singular or plural? What is your proof?

Formulate a rule to cover this situation. Be prepared to defend your wording, and, after a class consensus, write the rule here and in B104 as Rule 9.

B73. Let's add to the structured overview started in B19 and further developed in B34 and B47. First, fill in the spaces with the words used in B47. The following words or their abbreviations have been inserted as headings under *noun*: *singular, plural, singular and plural.* If the following words can be used as subjects, place them (or abbreviations thereof) in the boxes under the proper headings: *board of directors, women, five days, fifty dollars, to run, Gone with the Wind, measles, audience, oxen, trees, there,* and *person.*

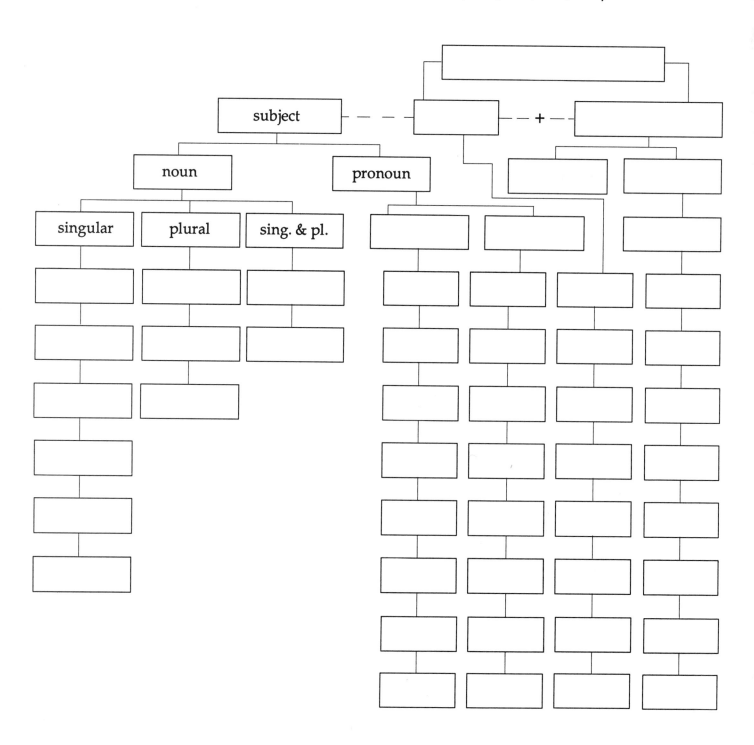

Be prepared to defend your placement of each of the terms in the structured overview in a class discussion. Note here any important points made during the class discussion.

PRACTICE

B74. In the following sentences, perform each of the first three steps of the subject/verb agreement process. (Look up the steps if you are not sure of them.) Finally, in the column on the left, place the rule number from B104 which supports the singular or plural characteristic of the subject. (Do not choose the verb yet!)

Rule #

A) Many English courses in the university system [attempts, attempt] to develop your writing ability.

B) The women in the management division [walks, walk] every day after work.

C) There [is, are] the committee to handle such problems.

D) Mathematics, of all the academic subjects, [is, are] stressed quite heavily in that school.

E) The board of directors [was, were] divided over the issue.

F) Five hundred dollars [is, are] a lot of money.

G) These scissors [cuts, cut] well.

H) Of all the law firms in town, only Fritz, Anderson, and Weiss [handles, handle] workman's comp cases.

I) To run every other day [are, is] important to my health.

Be prepared to defend your answers in a class discussion. Note here any important points made during the class discussion.

CLASSIFYING

B75. Nouns are not the only part of speech that create difficulty when you have to determine whether the word is singular or plural. Pronouns also have this difficulty.

Here's an example: In B38, we asked you to list the personal pronouns that could be used as subjects. Place that list of pronouns below.

SINGULAR   PLURAL

B76. *You* appears on both the singular and plural side of your list. According to your textbook and for purposes of subject/verb agreement, is *you* considered singular or plural or both?

On which page is this information found?

Formulate a rule to cover this situation. Be prepared to defend your wording, and, after a class consensus, write the rule here and in B104 as Rule 10.

B77. *You* also has another distinction besides its plural characteristic. It also is the subject of the following sentence.

Turn out the lights when leaving.

PREDICTING

How, you might ask, is *you* the subject of that sentence? Try to devise a rule to cover the situation.

FINDING PROOF

Find the rule for this in your text and compare it to yours.

DISCUSSING

B78. Discuss your comparison of rules with the class and note here any important points made during the class discussion.

(NOTE: This is not the last time you will encounter a missing, but understood, word in English grammar. More are coming in Topics C and D!)

B79. *I* is obviously singular. But for subject/verb agreement purposes, it is considered plural when used with present tense action verbs but not in all cases with *be* verbs. You will get a detailed explanation of the exceptions in B109. At this point however, place the following in B104 as Rule 11: <u>When *I* is the subject, place a "P" in the margin when used with action verbs and a "?" when used with *be* verbs.</u>

```
┌─────────────────────────────────────────┐
│  ┌────────────────────────────────────┐ │
│  │  TEST A PREDICTION - A             │ │
│  │  STEP-BY-STEP PROCESS              │ │
│  └────────────────────────────────────┘ │
└─────────────────────────────────────────┘
```

PREDICTING

B80. Indefinite pronouns also present a problem. Without looking in your textbook, classify those indefinite pronouns you listed in B43 as singular or plural.

SINGULAR   PLURAL

FINDING PROOF

B81. Locate in your reference text the page which indicates which of the indefinite pronouns you listed in B43 are singular and which are plural. Were you surprised to find that there is a third category of these pronouns, those that can be <u>either singular or plural?</u> Classify below indefinite pronouns as singular, plural, or either as your textbook does.

SINGULAR   PLURAL   EITHER

On which page is this information found?

```
┌─────────────────────────────────────────┐
│  ┌────────────────────────────────────┐ │
│  │  YOUR "HOW TO REMEMBER" SYSTEM     │ │
│  └────────────────────────────────────┘ │
└─────────────────────────────────────────┘
```

CREATING

B82. Compare your list of singular indefinite pronouns (B80) with the textbook's list of singular indefinite pronouns (B81). Possibly, you considered certain words to be plural, i.e. *everyone* and *everybody*. These words are in fact singular. Make up a rule or system that you can use to help you remember which indefinite pronouns are singular and which are plural.

B83. Compare your rule or system with other classmates and discuss and analyze each. Note interesting points here.

Formulate a rule to cover this situation. Be prepared to defend your wording, and, after a class consensus, write the rule here and in B104 as Rule 12. (The rule for those indefinite pronouns that are both singular and plural will be dealt with separately.)

```
┌─────────────────────────────┐
│  ┌───────────────────────┐  │
│  │ TEST A PREDICTION – A │  │
│  │ STEP-BY-STEP PROCESS  │  │
│  └───────────────────────┘  │
└─────────────────────────────┘
```

B84. As you have seen, another tricky aspect of indefinite pronouns is those pronouns that can be either singular or plural. Look at these two sentences:

    a. All of the report [is, are] finished.
    b. All of the reports [is, are] finished.

PREDICTING

In one of those sentences, the subject *all* is singular; in the other, it is plural. Other such indefinite pronouns are *most, some, half, part*. Generate a rule to explain how to know when these particular indefinite pronouns are singular and when they are plural.

Does the prepositional phrase that follows the subject play any role in determining whether the indefinite pronoun is singular or plural?

If yes, explain the role of the prepositional phrase.

FINDING PROOF

B85. Using your own text, copy the rule that governs this situation.

On which page is this information found?

B86. Compare your rule and the text's. Which rule is the most useful, which produces the most insight into the problem? Support your answer.

COMPARING

Formulate an appropriate rule to cover this situation. Be prepared to defend your wording and, after a class consensus, write the rule here and in B104 as Rule 13.

B87. Continuing our inquiry into singular and plural subjects, let's determine what happens in a sentence like this:

Jane and John, in addition to the girls in the fifth grade classes, [is, are] going to the school play.

a. Cross out the prepositional phrases.
b. Circle the subject.

B88. If you circled Jane and John as the subjects, you are correct. Now determine <u>on your own</u> whether the subject *Jane and John* is singular or plural.

PREDICTING

Why did you pick that answer; what are your reasons?

EXPLAINING

```
• • • • • • • • • • • • • • • • • • • • • • • • • • •
•   ALERT!  TAKE A TIME-ELAPSED PICTURE       •
•   OF YOUR MIND, AGAIN!                       •
•                                              •
• • • • • • • • • • • • • • • • • • • • • • • • • • •
```

B89. Find in your textbook the rule that determines whether the subject *Jane and John* is singular or plural and write the rule here.

FINDING PROOF

On which page is this information found?

Formulate your own wording for this rule. Be prepared to defend your wording and, after a class consensus, write the rule here and in B104 as Rule 14.

B90. Write out the steps you took and places you looked in your textbook to find the answer to that last question.

STEP ONE:

STEP TWO:

STEP THREE:

STEP FOUR:

B91. You may have noticed in your reading to answer B89 that some subjects joined by *and* remain singular. For instance, ham and eggs is considered singular. Find the textbook rule that explains this situation and write the rule here.

On which page is this information found?

Formulate your own wording for this rule. Be prepared to defend your wording, and, after a class consensus, write the rule here and in B104 as Rule 15.

TEST A PREDICTION – A
STEP-BY-STEP PROCESS

B92. You've just explored the rules for two subjects joined by the coordinating conjunction *and*. Suppose, however, that you have two subjects joined by the coordinating conjunction *or*. Should there be a different rule? Look at the following sentences:

    a. John or the girls [is, are] going to the dance.
    b. The girls or John [is, are] going to the dance.

Without looking in your textbook, formulate a rule that would explain why sentence "a" has a plural subject, and sentence "b" has a singular subject?

B93. Find the textbook rule that covers this situation and write the rule here.

FINDING PROOF

On which page is this information found?

B94. Compare the rule you discovered in your text (in answer to B93) with the one you formulated (in answer to B92). Decide which is the most useful and explain why.

B95. Decide as a class the most useful and accurate wording for this rule and write it here and in B104 as Rule 16.

COMPLEX PROBLEMS – BREAK
THE PROBLEM INTO PARTS

B96. Before a review of singular and plural nouns and pronouns, here is a mindbender for you. In B44, we determined that *each* can be used as an adjective (for example, "Each tree is tall.") or as an indefinite pronoun (for example, "Each of the trees is tall."). In B80 and B81, we found that when the indefinite pronoun *each* is used as a subject, it is considered singular (Rule 12). We also discovered in B87 – B89 that two subjects joined by *and* are plural (Rule 14). What happens, however, when *each and every* is used as an adjective before two subjects joined by *and*? Here's an example:

Each and every boy and girl [is, are] going to the movies.

Perform the following steps on this sentence:

    A. Cross out the prepositional phrase.
    B. Circle the subject.
    C. Determine if the subject is singular or plural.

B97. What does your textbook indicate the rule is for this situation?

On which page is this information found?

REMEMBERING

B98. How are you going to remember and use this rule?

Formulate an appropriate rule to cover this situation. Be prepared to defend your wording and, after a class consensus, write the rule here and in B104 as Rule 17.

PREDICTING

B99. Another problem with indefinite pronouns is created by the words *neither* and *either*. You discovered in B43 that *either* and *neither* are indefinite pronouns, and further discovered in B80 and B81 that they are considered singular (Rule 12). But these two words have another function that involves subjects, as exemplified by the following sentence:

Neither the boys nor the girl [walks, walk] to school.

Is the subject *neither* or *boys nor girl*?

FINDING PROOF

B100. What does your textbook indicate the subject should be?

On which page is this information found?

B101. If *boys nor girl* is the subject, is it singular or plural?

On which pages is this information found?

B102. What part of speech is the *neither. . . nor* combination considered to be, as it is used in the example sentence in B99?

On which page is this information found?

Formulate an appropriate rule to cover this situation. Be prepared to defend your wording, and, after a class consensus, write the rule here and in B104 as Rule 18.

B103. It's time to add to our ongoing structured overview. First duplicate the words in the structured overview in B73 here, <u>with these changes</u>: make sure you have examples of singular, plural, and singular and plural indefinite pronouns and indicate them with an "s," "p," or " s/p." Also indicate singular and plural subject pronouns with an "s" or "p." Finally, place these new words (or abbreviations) in the appropriate spaces: *tree and bush*, *colt or fillies*, *fillies or colt*, *each tree and bush*.

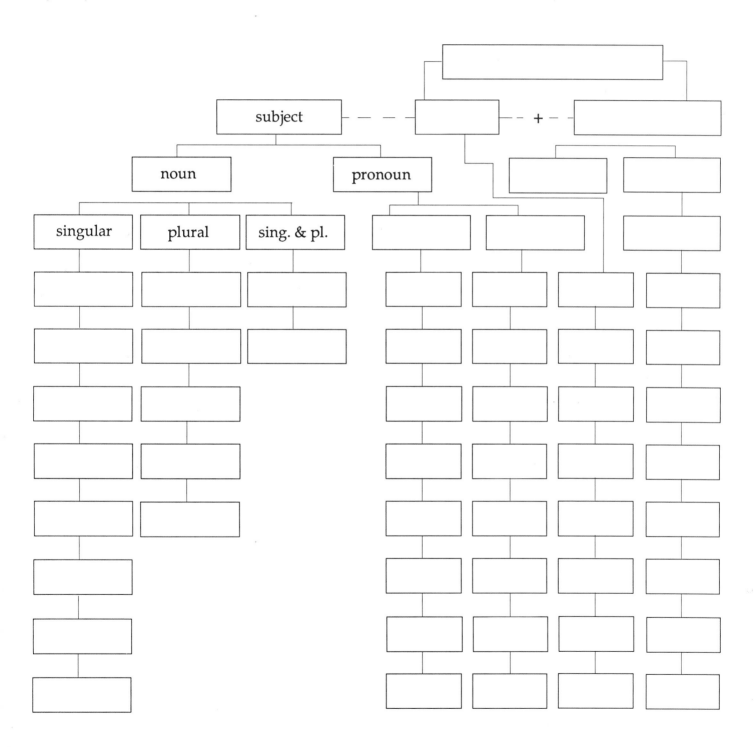

LISTING

B104. You should have collected here all the singular and plural subject rules for both nouns and pronouns discussed in this Topic. The rules that everyone in the class has written here should be consistent in both text and rule number.

1.

2.

3.

4.

5.

6.

7.

8.

9.

10.

11.

12.

13.

14.

15.

16.

17.

18.

B105. Your instructor will assign you subject/verb agreement sentences from your text. Perform the following steps on each of the sentences:

1. Cross out prepositional phrases.

2. Circle the subject(s).

3. If the circled subject is singular, place an "s" in the margin; if plural, place a "p" in the margin.

4. Write the Rule number (from the list you compiled in answer to question B104) that supports your decision as to whether the subject is singular or plural.

5. Do not choose the correct verb at this point.

Be prepared to perform each of these steps on all the sentences in class. Discuss any and all questions that arise. This step-by-step process is an excellent diagnostic tool to determine your grammar weaknesses, if any. If you missed an aspect of the subject/verb agreement process consistently (for instance not picking out all the prepositional phrases or not always determining the correct subject), then study this study guide and your textbook for that particular problem. Learn from your incorrect answers; they are not mistakes, they are opportunities to learn! Then do another set of exercises using the the same steps outlined above.

> ... CHECK IT OUT AGAIN! ...

PROOFREADING

B106. Using the essay you wrote in B11 in which you have already crossed out prepositional phrases and circled subjects, indicate whether each of your circled subjects is singular or plural and cite the Rule number from B104 to support your answer. Hand your essay in to your instructor who will circle two sentences. Be prepared to place those sentences on the board (without the steps indicated). Instruct your classmates to perform each of the three steps and, in addition, to determine the Rule number from B104 that supports the singular or plural subject choice.

> THE FINAL STEP, FINALLY!

APPLYING

B107. You will be glad to know that (1) you are now ready, after all this time, to choose the correct verb, and (2) this is the easiest part of the process! The fourth and final step in the procedure is:

STEP FOUR: IF YOU HAVE AN "S" IN THE MARGIN (BECAUSE THE SUBJECT IS SINGULAR), THE VERB SHOULD ALSO END IN "S"; IF YOU HAVE A "P" IN THE MARGIN (BECAUSE THE SUBJECT IS PLURAL), THE VERB SHOULD NOT END IN "S".

Now try all four steps on the following two sentences:

a. Many English courses in the university system [attempt, attempts] to develop your writing ability.

b. The committee [were, was] divided over the issue.

HOW DO YOU HANDLE EXCEPTIONS?

ANALYZING

B108. Before you apply this rule to the verbs in B36, B74, and the sentences you did from your text in response to B105, there are two exceptions that you should know about. The first is what happens when both versions of the verb end in "s," as in the following example.

Sally [dress, dresses] well.

Which verb is correct and what is your proof?

RESEARCHING

B109. The second exception involves the pronoun subject *I*. In Rule 11 (B104), you discovered that *I* as a subject is considered plural for subject/verb agreement purposes with action verbs but not always with *be* verbs. In order to work through this situation, place the correct forms of each verb opposite the nominative pronouns listed.

Be - Present tense

I	WE
YOU	YOU
HE	THEY
SHE	
IT	

Be - Past tense

I	WE
YOU	YOU
HE	THEY
SHE	
IT	

On which pages is this information found?

B110. Which pronoun/verb combinations follow the Fourth Step in the subject/verb process (that is, the subject is singular and the verb ends in "s") and which do not?

B111. How would you revise the wording of Rule 11 (B104) to take into account the specific problems of *I* as a subject with *be* verbs?

As a class, reach agreement on the wording and place the revised rule here and in B104 as revised Rule 11.

PRACTICE

B112. Now return to the sentences that you were assigned in B36, B74, and B105 and pick the correct verb in each according to the fourth and final step of the subject/verb agreement process. Be aware of the exceptions! (Also indicate the Rule number that supports why the subject is singular or plural if that has not already been done.)

Discuss the sentences, if any, that do not fit the Singular/Plural Subject Rules you have listed in B104. For each new situation encountered, look up the answers in your research text and be prepared to suggest a new Singular/Plural Subject Rule. Note here all new rules and add them to B104.

KEEP THE SUBJECT/VERB RULE STRAIGHT

B113. Is the following true: *The subject of a sentence must agree with its verb in number?* _____ Why or why not?

What is your proof?

Discuss this question with the class. Note here any points that interest you from the class discussion.

DISCUSSING

MORE DIFFICULT PRACTICE

B114. Here is an activity that is more difficult because you are not given a verb choice. In the following paragraph, some verbs are correct in their agreement with their subjects; others are not correct. Follow the four step process in <u>each</u> sentence. Change those verbs that are not correct; underline the verbs that are correct. Write in the margin the Singular/Plural Subject Rule number (from B104) for each of the circled subjects.

You, together with each classmate, is using thinking skills to learn English grammar. The theory behind these exercises are that you learn both thinking skills and English grammar. Everyone, including your teachers, have had much drill and application of isolated rules. Every English class have gone through a study of parts of speech. We were lectured on a rule and was then told to correct twenty sentences. There were no discussion. <u>Thinking Your Way Through English Grammar</u> attempt to focus on the relationships of all the terms. But most important, you have been put in a situation where you, and not your teacher, is responsible for your own learning.

...AND CHECK IT OUT, AGAIN!

B115. Refer to the essay you wrote in B11 in which you have already completed the first three steps of the subject/verb agreement process. Now it is time to make sure you have used the correct verb form. Some of the verbs in your essay may not be present tense verbs or don't have helping verbs, which means they don't present subject/verb agreement problems. Underline all the verbs in your essay and, using the fourth step, correct the present tense or helping verbs that are incorrect. Bracket the verbs that are correctly used. Be prepared to conduct class on individual sentences from your essay as your instructor may indicate.

PROOFREADING

LISTING

B116. In your own words, restate the process that this study guide has required you to follow in attacking subject/verb agreement problems.

STEP ONE:

STEP TWO:

STEP THREE:

STEP FOUR:

EVALUATING

B117. Evaluate the process.

Is it helpful?

What do you like or not like about it?

Any other observations.

THINKING

B118. This four step subject/verb agreement process is just one way to study this subject. You are capable of thinking of your own way to solve such problems. Think about it! Write your process here.

STEP ONE:

STEP TWO:

STEP THREE:

STEP FOUR:

STEP FIVE:

B119. Discuss your answers to the last three questions with the rest of the
class. Note here points of interest you want to remember.

DISCUSSING

┌─────────────────────────────────┐
│ ANSWER YOUR QUESTIONS   │
└─────────────────────────────────┘

B120. In question B9, we asked you to list (but not answer) a series of
questions that you were interested in answering as you read through the
material in this study guide and your textbook. Answer those questions
now.

ANSWER TO QUESTION 1.

ANSWER TO QUESTION 2.

ANSWER TO QUESTION 3.

B121. Going as deeply into a subject as you have should not only answer questions you posed earlier, but might also raise new ones. Developing analytical skills can produce a curiosity to learn and your reference skills can satisfy that curiosity. List any new questions that arise out of subject/verb agreement and indicate how you would approach finding answers to them.

QUESTION 1.

QUESTION 2.

QUESTION 3.

DISCUSSING

B122. Discuss your questions and reference approaches in class and note here any points of interest.

TOPIC C:
STRATEGIC THINKING WITH PRONOUNS

The goal of Topic C is for you, the student, to develop analytical thinking strategies to solve pronoun problems. In addition, these analytical thinking strategies will be used to determine major sentence functions as well: subject, direct object, etc. In an even broader context, the thinking that you are specifically required to use to form these analytical pronoun and function strategies can be the basis to develop analytical thinking strategies to solve other, non-grammatical, problems as well.

Developing strategies to solve grammatical problems reinforces the underlying theme here: that English grammar is an interweaving of related concepts for which you can develop strategies to help create effective communication, just as a weaver develops a strategy to blend threads together to form a tapestry. The complexity of the English language is further seen, not as a series of rigid rules, but as a very flexible, ingenious, and beautiful system over which you have control.

The format of this Topic remains the same. Pronoun problems are presented, through a series of questions, as a puzzle for you to solve or a tapestry for you to construct. The concept of using your text as a reference book is also retained: problems are assigned, not page numbers. Please feel free to explore your text as you generate questions. Also don't forget the glossary you developed in Topic A. Add to it as new words and concepts are introduced.

Topic C will continue those "Check It Out!..." exercises introduced in Topic B where you were required to review your own written work for the grammatical problems you have explored. Remember, you are learning to think in the context of grammar so you can review your own writing to make it grammatically correct and properly understood.

C1. Your first assignment in this Topic is to write a 100 word paragraph in which you describe a friend whom you find to be particularly humorous. Try to use as many pronouns as possible. The paragraph should be triple spaced.

```
┌─────────────────────┐
│   PRONOUN CHOICES    │
└─────────────────────┘
```

ANALYZING

C2. Each of the following sentences gives you pronoun choices. Do not pick the pronoun! Instead, think! Using your knowledge of the characteristics of pronouns you studied in Topics A and B, determine if there is a pattern to the <u>kinds of pronouns</u> from which you are to choose. (You will get to choose the correct pronoun later, for these sentences are used throughout this Topic to organize your study of function strategies and pronoun problems.)

A. Sally will go to the movies with (they, them).

B. (He, Him) will go to the movies with them.

C. It was (I, me) who had seen this movie.

D. It hit (I, me) in the face.

E. Cynthia and (he, him) are also going to the movies with Mary and (I, me).

F. The class elected two representatives, Joshua and (I, me), to the Student Government Association.

G. Two representatives, Joshua and (I, me), were elected to the Student Government Association.

H. (We, Us) football players practice hard everyday in the fall.

I. The football coach tells (we, us) players to practice hard in the spring, too.

J. The jacket looks better on you than (I, me).

K. Frank ran a better race than (he, him).

Between what two characteristics (or kinds) of pronouns do these pronoun choices require you to choose?

EXPLAINING

C3. In general, are you analyzing a sentence for part of speech, characteristic, or function when you have to determine whether the nominative or the objective pronoun is the correct choice? Be prepared to defend your answer.

A large part of this Topic will be devoted to developing the strategies required to determine the <u>function</u> the pronoun performs in a sentence. Having first determined <u>function</u>, you can then choose the correct pronoun characteristic for that function.

A REVIEW

C4. In B21, you were asked to name four functions a noun or pronoun can perform in a sentence. As a review, here is that same structured overview used in B21 with the addition of a fifth function. Fill in the five major functions a noun or pronoun can perform in a sentence in the first row of boxes.

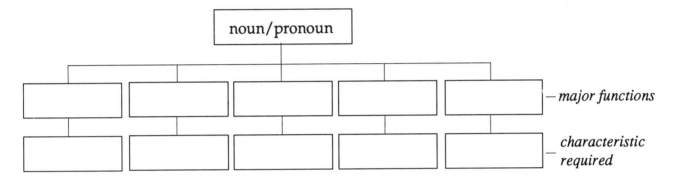

C5. Now list the characteristic (nominative or objective) of the pronoun required for each function in the boxes below the named function.

On which pages is this information found?

C6. List the nominative personal pronouns and the objective personal pronouns.

Nominative		Objective	
sing.	plural	sing.	plural

On which pages is this information found?

OBJECT OF A PREPOSITION STRATEGY

C7. From your work on the four step subject/verb agreement process in Topic B, you already know the strategies to find two functions: that is, determining when a pronoun is functioning (1) as an object of a preposition, and (2) as a subject of a sentence.

Concentrating on the object of a preposition function first, let's review from your glossary (A4) some of the basic terms. Define the following words:

PREPOSITION

OBJECT OF A PREPOSITION

PREPOSITIONAL PHRASE

PROBLEM-SOLVING

C8. Here is a sentence containing a prepositional phrase:

Sally will go to the movies with (they, them).

Think about how you find prepositional phrases and how you determine whether a pronoun is functioning as the object of a preposition.

Develop a strategy that would help you pick out prepositional phrases and determine if a pronoun is functioning as an object of a preposition. Your OBJECT OF A PREPOSITION STRATEGY should be as complete and detailed as possible and should include, at a minimum, references to prepositions, to the definition of prepositional phrases, and to the characteristics of personal pronouns required as an object of a preposition. (If you have not completed Topic B or need a quick review, please do [or review] exercises B21 through B31 before attempting to formulate this strategy.)

One final instruction on developing these strategies. The five steps below are just a guide. Write as many or as few steps as you feel is necessary. Use the margins if more space is required.

STEP ONE:

STEP TWO:

STEP THREE:

STEP FOUR:

STEP FIVE:

C9.   Use your OBJECT OF A PREPOSITION STRATEGY to determine the correct pronoun in the following sentence:

> Sally will go to the movies with (they, them).

Give the reasons for your choice.

You will have more practice with your OBJECT OF A PREPOSITION STRATEGY after a review of the SUBJECT STRATEGY discussed next.

SUBJECT STRATEGY

C10.   You have just developed the first of your FUNCTION STRATEGIES, the OBJECT OF A PREPOSITION STRATEGY.   Now you'll explore the second, the SUBJECT STRATEGY.   First, define:

SUBJECT

C11.   Think about how you determine which word is the subject of a sentence and whether the pronoun in question is functioning as the subject of the sentence.

Develop a strategy that would help you determine if a pronoun is functioning as a subject of a sentence.   Your SUBJECT STRATEGY should be as complete and detailed as possible and should include, at a minimum, references to prepositional phrases, to the definition of subjects, to the use of verbs to find subjects, and to the type of personal pronouns required to be subjects of a sentence.   (Use as many steps as you think you need.)

STEP ONE:

STEP TWO:

STEP THREE:

STEP FOUR:

STEP FIVE:

C12. Using your SUBJECT STRATEGY, go through each of the steps you developed in C11 and circle the correct pronoun in the following sentence:

(He, Him) will go to the movies with them.

Give the reasons for your answer.

There are, of course, other kinds of pronouns that can act as the subject of a sentence. This Topic does not deal with them all, only the ones that are most frequently tested.

C13. These next few questions integrate the two FUNCTION STRATEGIES you have just developed. When you examined prepositions in Topic B, you discovered that many prepositions are also other parts of speech. For instance, you discovered that *to* plus a verb is not a prepositional phrase but is a verbal called an infinitive. *Below* is both a preposition and an adverb. The following prepositions are also other parts of speech and create some especially troublesome pronoun problems. Name the other part of speech of the following prepositions:

since _____ but _____ for_____

Here is the problem. When these words function as prepositions (i.e., "Everyone went but him."), then the pronoun following would be the object of a preposition and be in the objective case. However, when these words function as coordinating or subordinating conjunctions, (i.e., "Everyone went, but he didn't.") the pronoun following functions as _____.

C14. In the following sentences, (1) determine and name the part of speech of the underlined word, (2) state the function of the pronoun that follows, (3) name the characteristic of the pronoun needed to perform that function, and (4) circle the correct form of the pronoun.

a. Mary has stopped visiting friends <u>since</u> (he, him) came into her life.

PART OF SPEECH OF UNDERLINED WORD:

FUNCTION OF FOLLOWING PRONOUN:

PRONOUN CHARACTERISTIC NEEDED:

b. Everyone <u>but</u> (she, her) went to the movies.

PART OF SPEECH OF UNDERLINED WORD:

FUNCTION OF FOLLOWING PRONOUN:

PRONOUN CHARACTERISTIC NEEDED:

c. Everyone is still here, <u>but</u> (she, her) went to the movies.

PART OF SPEECH OF UNDERLINED WORD:

FUNCTION OF FOLLOWING PRONOUN:

PRONOUN CHARACTERISTIC NEEDED:

d. This is the best thing <u>for</u> (she, her).

PART OF SPEECH OF UNDERLINED WORD:

FUNCTION OF FOLLOWING PRONOUN:

PRONOUN CHARACTERISTIC NEEDED:

e. This could be the best thing, <u>for</u> (she, her) can now take both courses.

PART OF SPEECH OF UNDERLINED WORD:

FUNCTION OF FOLLOWING PRONOUN:

PRONOUN CHARACTERISTIC NEEDED:

C15. State in your own words how you went about determining whether the words *since, but,* or *for* were used as prepositions or as another part of speech in these sentences.

EXPLAINING

C16. How do the multiple parts of speech of these (and other) prepositions affect the OBJECT OF A PREPOSITION STRATEGY developed in C8?

EVALUATING

> . . . AND CHECK IT OUT! . . .

C17. Now get out the paragraph you wrote in C1. Using each step in your OBJECT OF A PREPOSITION STRATEGY, underline each object of a preposition. Place a "P" or an "N" over the object to indicate pronoun or noun, respectively. Correct any pronouns that are used incorrectly.

PROOFREADING

Using each step of your SUBJECT STRATEGY, circle each subject. Place a "P" or an "N" over the subject to indicate pronoun or noun respectively. Correct any pronouns that are used incorrectly. Be prepared to write some of your sentences on the board and lead the class in a discussion.

C18. To integrate your learning about the function terms of object of preposition and subject with characteristics and parts of speech, here is a structured overview that requires you to use the strategies just developed. Label the part of speech of the word in the boxes directly above the word, characteristics of the word in the boxes above the parts of speech, and the function the word performs below the word.

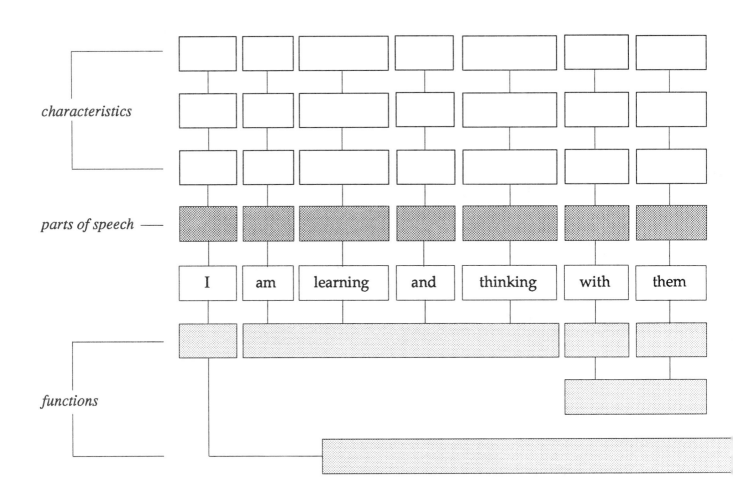

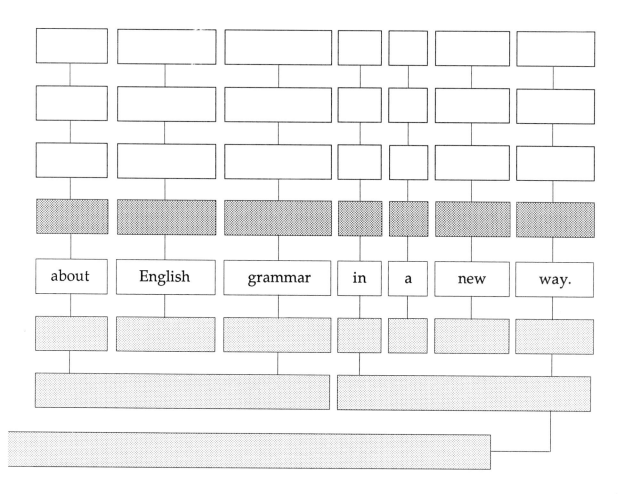

about   English   grammar   in   a   new   way.

RESEARCHING

C19. A difficult pronoun function problem is determining whether a pronoun following a verb functions as a predicate nominative or as a direct or indirect object. The problem is created by the fact that a nominative pronoun is required for one of the functions and an objective pronoun is required for the others. The confusing situation is further compounded by the fact that you might be accustomed to hearing a different form of the pronoun used for a predicate nominative than is required in formal, written English. The following sentences illustrate this problem:

It was (I, me) who had seen this movie.

It hit (I, me) in the face.

Before developing a strategy for the predicate nominative/direct object functions, make sure you understand the definitions of some terms. Define the following terms and indicate the characteristic of the personal pronoun required to perform that function.

PREDICATE NOMINATIVE

DIRECT OBJECT

INDIRECT OBJECT

On which pages is this information found?

RESEARCHING

C20. Have you discovered in your research that it is the verb that dictates whether a predicate nominative or a direct/indirect object will follow? What kind of verb characteristic signals that a predicate nominative (or predicate adjective) might follow?

On which pages is this information found?

Name as many verbs with this characteristic as you can.

On which pages is this information found?

C21. What kind of verb characteristic signals that a direct or indirect object might follow?

On which pages is this information found?

Name as many verbs with this characteristic as you can.

On which pages is this information found?

C22. Let's put all this information together. Develop a strategy that would help you determine if a pronoun following a verb is functioning as a predicate nominative or direct/indirect object. Your PREDICATE NOMINATIVE/DIRECT OBJECT/ INDIRECT OBJECT STRATEGY should be as complete and detailed as possible and should include, at a minimum, references to the definitions of predicate nominatives and direct/indirect objects and to the characteristics of the verbs and the pronouns required for each. (Use as many steps as needed.)

STEP ONE:

STEP TWO:

STEP THREE:

STEP FOUR:

STEP FIVE:

C23. Using each step of your PREDICATE NOMINATIVE/DIRECT OBJECT/INDIRECT OBJECT STRATEGY, (1) determine the characteristic of the verb, (2) determine the function of the pronoun following, (3) determine the characteristic of the pronoun required, and (4) circle the correct pronoun in the following sentences.

It was (I, me) who had seen this movie.

CHARACTERISTIC OF THE VERB:
FUNCTION OF THE FOLLOWING PRONOUN:
PRONOUN CHARACTERISTIC NEEDED:

It hit (I, me) in the face.

CHARACTERISTIC OF THE VERB:
FUNCTION OF THE FOLLOWING PRONOUN:
PRONOUN CHARACTERISTIC NEEDED:

Here is some practice with nouns (instead of pronouns) performing the predicate nominative/ direct object functions. Determine the function of the underlined words in each sentence below. Be prepared to defend your answers by reference to your PREDICATE NOMINATIVE/DIRECT OBJECT/INDIRECT OBJECT STRATEGY.

a.   Eric is hitting the <u>student</u>.

b.   Eric is a <u>student</u>.

c.   Janette is a <u>cheerleader</u>.

d.   Janette is giving a <u>cheerleader</u> the pin.

e.   Ike was the <u>captain</u> of the team

f.   Ike told the <u>captain</u> the new plays.

> ANALYZE A SENTENCE: PARTS OF SPEECH,
> CHARACTERISTICS, AND FUNCTIONS

C24. Let's have some fun with direct and indirect objects. These sentences are identical. However, their meaning can be changed by changing the function certain words in the sentences perform, without changing the words themselves! Label the parts of speech (in the boxes directly above the word), characteristics (above the parts of speech), and functions (below the words) for each sentence to achieve different meanings for the sentences. Notice how the part of speech and characteristics of a word change as the function of the word changes.

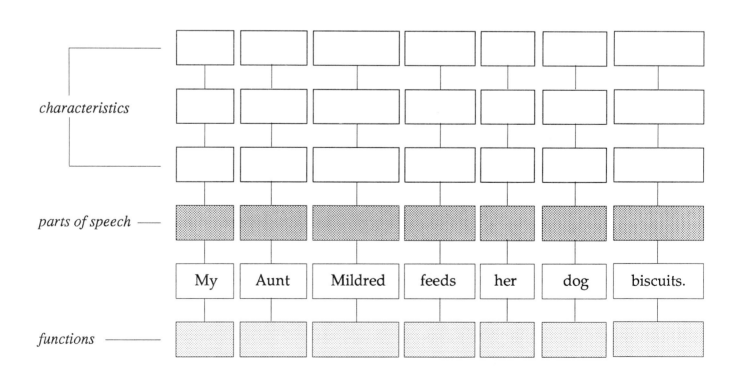

characteristics

parts of speech ——

| My | Aunt | Mildred | feeds | her | dog | biscuits. |

functions ——

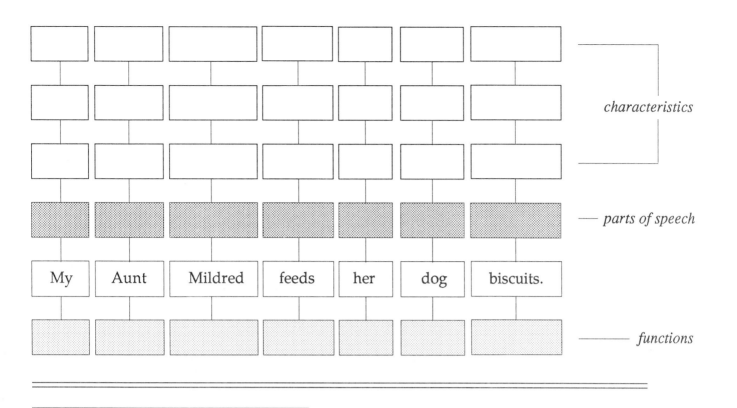

characteristics

parts of speech

| My | Aunt | Mildred | feeds | her | dog | biscuits. |

functions

┌─────────────────────────────┐
│ ... CHECK IT OUT AGAIN! ... │
└─────────────────────────────┘

C25. Now get out the paragraph you wrote in C1. Using each step in your PREDICATE NOMINATIVE/DIRECT OBJECT/INDIRECT OBJECT STRATEGY, underline and label all predicate nominatives, direct objects, and indirect objects, both noun and pronoun. Also place a "P" or an "N" over the underlined word to indicate pronoun or noun, respectively. Correct any pronouns that are used incorrectly.

Be prepared to write any of your sentences on the board and conduct a class discussion on them.

PROOFREADING

┌─────────────────────────────┐
│ DON'T COMPOUND THE PROBLEM   │
└─────────────────────────────┘

C26. You'll be happy to know that you have reviewed your last major function strategy. The next four pronoun problems discussed are just variations of the FUNCTION STRATEGIES you've just developed. These variations build on the knowledge you have just learned — they are not exceptions — so you will have to continue to use those FUNCTION STRATEGIES you have developed.

The first variation is compound functions, which seem to create pronoun problems when in fact they should not. Let's examine what the problems might be and devise a strategy to think clearly through compound functions to avoid those problems.

The following sentence illustrates the point.

> Cynthia and (he, him) are also going to the movies with Mary and (I, me).

Before developing a strategy to think your way through compound functions, answer the following questions:

What are compound functions (sometimes called compound constructions) and how are they formed?

On which pages is this information found?

C27. What part of speech is required to make words or phrases compound?

List examples of that part of speech here:

On which pages is this information found?

ANALYZING

C28. Does the fact that a word or phrase is compound change its function in a sentence?

Does the fact that the sentence has a compound subject mean that a nominative pronoun should not be used as the subject?

Does the fact that the sentence contains a compound object of a preposition mean that an objective pronoun should not be used as the object of a preposition?

RESEARCHING

What material from the text can you use to support your answers, giving quotes, if any, and pages numbers.

BEING AWARE

C29. Using the definitions and the insights from the three previous questions, now choose the correct pronouns in the sentence that opened this discussion. As you do this task, be aware of what your mind is doing to pick the proper pronouns in compound word situations. These steps would necessarily include being aware (1) of the FUNCTION STRATEGIES you are using to find the function of the compound constructions, and (2) of the characteristics of the pronoun performing that function.

                        1.
        Cynthia and (he, him) are also going to the movies with Mary
              2.
        and (I, me).

FUNCTION OF THE COMPOUND WORDS:

1.
2.

PRONOUN CHARACTERISTIC NEEDED:

1.
2.

Support the reasons for your answers with reference to your FUNCTION STRATEGIES.

PROBLEM-SOLVING

C30. How will you deal with compound constructions in the FUNCTION STRATEGIES you have already developed? Devise a strategy that would take compound construction into consideration in your FUNCTION STRATEGIES.

STEP ONE:

STEP TWO:

STEP THREE:

STEP FOUR:

STEP FIVE:

PRACTICE

ANALYZING

C31. Here are some sentences, many of which contain pronoun choices in compound situations. Using all the FUNCTION STRATEGIES you have developed together with your compound construction strategy, choose the correct pronoun by (1) naming the function the pronoun choice performs in the sentence, and (2) stating the pronoun characteristic required for that function.

a.   The choice is between John and (I, me).

      FUNCTION OF THE PRONOUN:
      PRONOUN CHARACTERISTIC NEEDED:

b.   Judy and (I, me) are going to the movies.

      FUNCTION OF THE PRONOUN:
      PRONOUN CHARACTERISTIC NEEDED:

c.   Tara and (I, me) saw that movie again.

      FUNCTION OF THE PRONOUN:
      PRONOUN CHARACTERISTIC NEEDED:

d.   It was George and (I, me) who went to the store.

FUNCTION OF THE PRONOUN:
PRONOUN CHARACTERISTIC NEEDED:

e.   Lisa gave George and (I, me) a present.

FUNCTION OF THE PRONOUN:
PRONOUN CHARACTERISTIC NEEDED:

                                             1.   2.

f.   The winners of all the prizes were (she, her) and (he, him).

1. FUNCTION OF THE PRONOUN:
PRONOUN CHARACTERISTIC NEEDED:

2. FUNCTION OF THE PRONOUN:
PRONOUN CHARACTERISTIC NEEDED:

g.   The family has known my brothers and (I, me) for ten years.

FUNCTION OF THE PRONOUN:
PRONOUN CHARACTERISTIC NEEDED:

                        1.   2.   3.

h.   Jack described (they, them) to (she, her) and (I, me).

1. FUNCTION OF THE PRONOUN:
PRONOUN CHARACTERISTIC NEEDED:

2. FUNCTION OF THE PRONOUN:
PRONOUN CHARACTERISTIC NEEDED:

3. FUNCTION OF THE PRONOUN:
PRONOUN CHARACTERISTIC NEEDED:

i.   Frank does not want to go since (he, him) had seen the movie before.

FUNCTION OF THE PRONOUN:
PRONOUN CHARACTERISTIC NEEDED:

j.   Frank has dated many girls since (she, her).

FUNCTION OF THE PRONOUN:
PRONOUN CHARACTERISTIC NEEDED:

                             1.   2.

k.   Her mother did everything for (she, her), for (she, her) was very sick.

1. FUNCTION OF THE PRONOUN:
PRONOUN CHARACTERISTIC NEEDED:

2. FUNCTION OF THE PRONOUN:
PRONOUN CHARACTERISTIC NEEDED:

C32. Here is the second variation to the FUNCTION STRATEGIES you have explored so far. At first, you will be learning that the appositive is a new function, but you will also soon see how it relates to the SUBJECT, OBJECT OF PREPOSITION, and PREDICATE NOMINATIVE/OBJECT STRATEGIES previously developed.

The appositive variation arises in sentences like the following:

> The class elected two representatives, Joshua and (I, me), to the Student Government Association.

> Two representatives, Joshua and (I, me), were elected to the Student Government Association.

Did you define *appositive* in your personal glossary in A4? Check back and/or look up the definition and recopy it here.

DEFINING

C33. In sentence G, *Joshua and me* is correct. In sentence H, *Joshua and I* is correct. Formulate a reason that you can use to explain these pronoun choices.

PREDICTING

C34. What material from the text can you use to support your answers, giving quotes, if any, and pages numbers.

RESEARCHING

C35. Using the definitions and the insights from the three previous questions, now choose the correct pronouns in the following sentences. As you do this task, be aware of what your mind is doing to pick the proper pronouns in appositive situations. This will necessarily include being aware (1) of the FUNCTION STRATEGIES you are using to determine the function of the word preceeding the appositive, and (2) of the characteristic of the pronoun that would perform such a function.

BEING AWARE

> The class elected two representatives, Joshua and (I, me), to the Student Government Association.

> FUNCTION OF THE WORD RENAMED BY THE APPOSITIVE:
> PRONOUN CHARACTERISTIC NEEDED:

> Two representatives, Joshua and (I, me), were elected to the Student Government Association.

> FUNCTION OF THE WORD RENAMED BY THE APPOSITIVE:
> PRONOUN CHARACTERISTIC NEEDED:

Support the reasons for your answers with reference to your FUNCTION STRATEGIES.

C36. How will you deal with appositives in the FUNCTION STRATEGIES you have already developed? Devise a strategy that would take appositives into consideration in your FUNCTIONS STRATEGIES.

STEP ONE:

STEP TWO:

STEP THREE:

STEP FOUR:

STEP FIVE:

C37. In the structured overview in C24, you analyzed how a sentence about Aunt Mildred's dog could be interpreted two ways. Here is the same sentence with only a change in punctuation and capitalization that produces a third meaning for this sentence! Explore your knowledge of appositives, together with parts of speech, characteristics of words, and word functions to achieve a third meaning for this very same sentence.

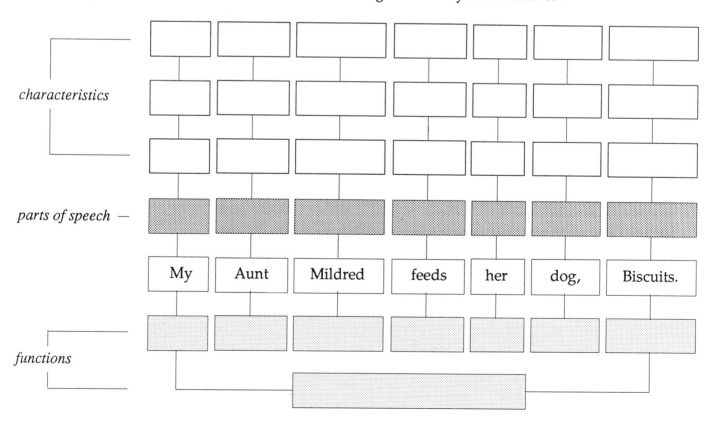

C38. Though the pronoun choices in the example sentences below are not called reverse appositives in the grammar texts, it certainly appears to be an appropriate name. Like appositives, these pronouns do rename or stand for a noun, but here, the pronouns come BEFORE, not after, the noun they rename. Another point of difference is that though both nouns and pronouns can be appositives, only pronouns can act as these reverse appositives. The following sentences are examples:

(We, Us) football players practice hard everyday in the fall.

The football coach tells (we, us) players to practice hard in the spring, too.

PREDICTING

Review the above two sentences and attempt to discover a relationship between the function of the pronoun and the function of the noun following. State your understanding of that relationship here.

RESEARCHING

C39. What material from the text can you use to support your answers, giving quotes, if any, and pages numbers.

BEING AWARE

C40. Using the observations and the insights from the three previous questions, choose the correct pronouns in the sentence that opened this discussion. As you do this task, be aware of what your mind is doing to pick the proper pronouns in reverse appositive situations. This would necessarily include being aware (1) of the FUNCTION STRATEGIES you are using to determine the function of the noun following the pronoun, and (2) of the characteristics of the pronoun that would perform that function.

(We, Us) football players practice hard everyday in the fall.

FUNCTION OF THE FOLLOWING NOUN:
PRONOUN CHARACTERISTIC NEEDED:

The football coach tells (we, us) players to practice hard in the spring, too.

FUNCTION OF THE FOLLOWING NOUN:
PRONOUN CHARACTERISTIC NEEDED:

Support the reasons for your answers with reference to your FUNCTION STRATEGIES.

PROBLEM-SOLVING

C41. State the steps you used to choose the pronouns in the above sentences, making reference to reverse appositives, the appropriate PRONOUN STRATEGIES, and pronoun characteristics. Be as specific as possible on ALL the steps and use as many steps as you need.

STEP ONE:

STEP TWO:

STEP THREE:

STEP FOUR:

STEP FIVE:

> THE FINAL VARIATION: A
> HIDDEN FUNCTION CHOICE

ANALYZING

C42. This last variation uses the SUBJECT and/or OBJECT FUNCTION STRATEGIES (which you have already developed) in unusual sentence structures. The following sentences contain a subject and an object function choice that is not obvious on initial examination.

1.   The jacket looks better on you than (I, me).

2.   Frank ran a better race than (he, him).

Figure out a way to use your OBJECT OF A PREPOSITION STRATEGY in sentence 1 to justify the objective pronoun *me* as the correct choice.

Figure out a way to use your SUBJECT STRATEGY in sentence 2 to justify the nominative pronoun *he* as the correct pronoun choice.

C43. How does your text express the rule that covers this problem?

On which pages is this information found?

C44. Based on your answers to the last two questions, develop a strategy to choose the correct pronoun in these hidden function situations. Use as many steps as necessary to have a useful process.

STEP ONE:

STEP TWO:

STEP THREE:

STEP FOUR:

STEP FIVE:

C45. You have probably discovered that the solution to these hidden function pronoun problems lies in the use of an unstated verb and/or preposition. What other "understood" or unstated word have you encountered in this study guide? (A hint: look in Topic B.)

C46. Before you leave this hidden function choice, you should be aware that these "unstated words" create a more serious problem. There are times when an unstated verb can be placed in a sentence so either the objective or subjective form of the pronoun could be used. Here is an example of such a sentence that illustrates this dilemma:

Lisa liked Jonathan as much as (he, him).

Rewrite the sentence by inserting the unstated verb (and other necessary words) so that *he* would be the correct pronoun choice.

Now rewrite the sentence by inserting the unstated verb (and other necessary words) so that *him* would be the correct pronoun choice.

C47. You have seen in the Aunt Mildred and her dog sentences (C24 and C37) the ambiguity nouns and pronouns can create. Now discuss the problems that unstated words create for pronoun choice.

```
. . . CHECK IT OUT AGAIN! . . .
```

PROOFREADING

C48. Go back through the paragraph you wrote in C1 and determine if your sentences contain any of these four variations (compound, appositive, reverse appositive, unstated words) just discussed. If yes, name the variation and determine, using the appropriate strategy you have developed, whether the pronoun (if any) was correctly used. Be prepared to lead a class discussion on your sentences.

```
PRACTICE
```

C49. In order to practice the methodology and strategies developed in this Topic, you will be required to analyze the following sentences in a highly structured way. This is done so you get some practice with this kind of analysis and so that the methodology becomes second nature to you. Keep in mind that you are learning both analytical skills <u>and</u> English grammar!

Here is what you will be required to do in class when called upon to analyze a sentence:

(1)   Determine the function of the pronoun and be prepared to explain the FUNCTION STRATEGY and the variation, if any, you used.

(2)   Name the characteristic of the pronoun used to perform that function.

(3)   Circle the correct pronoun.

ANALYZING

Keep in mind that the correct answer is not the only consideration here. Also important are: (A) the steps you took to come up with the answer, (B) your awareness of those steps, and (C) your articulation of your awareness.

Here is a model of some of the thoughts that might run through your mind as you search for an answer to the correct pronoun in this sentence:

"John gave Lisa and (I, me) some firewood for the winter season.

"Before checking through the possible functions for this pronoun choice, I notice the pronoun is part of a compound phrase. Using my compound pronoun variation, I will cross out "Lisa and" and not be distracted by a compound construction.

"I like to check through the possible functions in the order in which I learned them. The first function strategy I use is the OBJECT OF A PREPOSITION STRATEGY. I notice that the word 'for' is there. It is a preposition and not acting as a coordinating conjunction because there is no subject / verb combination following. So the only prepositional phrase in the sentence, 'for the winter season,' does not contain the pronoun in question.

"The next function I look for is the subject. Using my SUBJECT STRATEGY, I determine that the verb is 'gave' and the person or thing doing the giving is 'John.' 'John' is the subject of the sentence. The pronoun choice is therefore not the subject.

"The next function I look for is the PREDICATE NOMINATIVE/DIRECT OBJECT/INDIRECT OBJECT STRATEGY. I notice that the pronoun in question comes after the verb. [Of course, after this function analysis becomes second nature to you, you can go directly to this step, but the intent here is develop an orderly, systematic approach to the learning process.] That strategy requires I look at the verb. 'Gave' is an action verb; therefore the pronoun choice is going to be either a direct or indirect object.

"The direct object answers the question what was given, and in this sentence, 'firewood' was given so it is the direct object. The indirect object answers the question to whom or for whom was the direct object, 'firewood,' given. The pronoun choice in this sentence functions as the indirect object. The indirect object takes an objective pronoun, and 'me' is an objective pronoun so I will circle 'me.'"

a.   The choice is between Henry and (I, me).

FUNCTION OF PRONOUN IN QUESTION:

PRONOUN CHARACTERISTIC NEEDED:

b.   (She, her) and (I, me) are going to the movies tonight.

FUNCTION OF PRONOUNS IN QUESTION:

PRONOUN CHARACTERISTIC NEEDED:

c.   Tara and (I, me) saw that movie again.

FUNCTION OF PRONOUN IN QUESTION:

PRONOUN CHARACTERISTIC NEEDED:

d.   It was (I, me) who went to the store.

FUNCTION OF PRONOUN IN QUESTION:

PRONOUN CHARACTERISTIC NEEDED:

e. The runners, (she, her) and (I, me), had a good workout this morning.

   FUNCTION OF PRONOUNS IN QUESTION:

   PRONOUN CHARACTERISTIC NEEDED:

f. Russ and Billy are much more accomplished Bluegrass instrumentalists than (they, them).

   FUNCTION OF PRONOUN IN QUESTION:

   PRONOUN CHARACTERISTIC NEEDED:

g. (We, Us) students have to stick together on this issue.

   FUNCTION OF PRONOUN IN QUESTION:

   PRONOUN CHARACTERISTIC NEEDED:

h. The winner of prizes was (I, me).

   FUNCTION OF PRONOUN IN QUESTION:

   PRONOUN CHARACTERISTIC NEEDED:

i. The family has known my brothers and (I, me) for ten years.

   FUNCTION OF PRONOUN IN QUESTION:

   PRONOUN CHARACTERISTIC NEEDED:

j. We told the two waitresses, Judy and (she, her), that we had to leave early.

   FUNCTION OF PRONOUN IN QUESTION:

   PRONOUN CHARACTERISTIC NEEDED:

k. That suit looks better on you than (I, me).

   FUNCTION OF PRONOUN IN QUESTION:

   PRONOUN CHARACTERISTIC NEEDED:

C50. Analyze this sentence by labeling the part of speech, characteristics, and the functions for each word in the sentence.

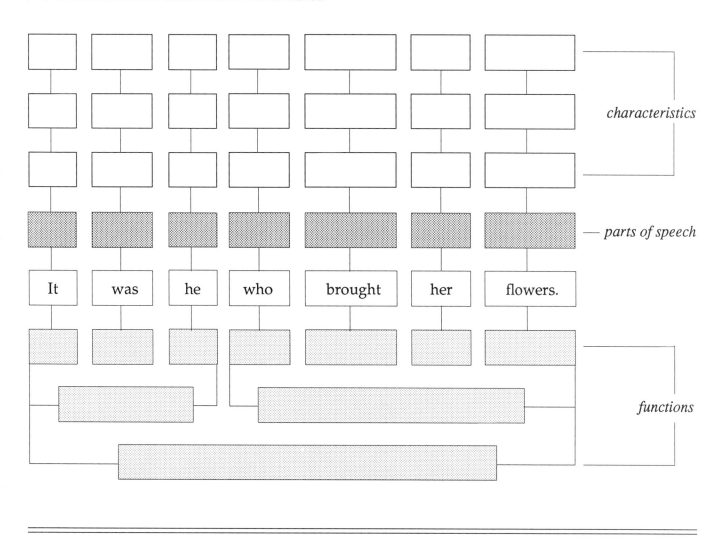

characteristics

— parts of speech

It   was   he   who   brought   her   flowers.

functions

C51. The first part of this Topic has explored the pronoun choices that involve the function the pronoun is performing in a sentence. In the sentences you are about to analyze, the correct pronoun does NOT depend on word function, but does depend on word characteristics. The following sentence illustrates the problem:

Every one of the students is going to (his, her, his/her, their) seat.

Between what two characteristics of a pronoun is this sentence asking you to choose when the choice is between *his* and *their*?

C52. What kind of pronouns are *his, her, their*?

On which pages is this information found?

C53. List the possessive personal pronouns in the spaces below. The first one is completed.

singular		plural
my	mine	

ANALYZING

C54. Just to put these unusual pronouns into an analytical context, state the FUNCTION that *my, your, his, her, its, our, your,* and *their* can perform in a sentence.

State the FUNCTIONS that *mine, yours, his, hers, its, ours, yours,* and *theirs* can perform in a sentence.

On which pages is this information found?

RESEARCHING

C55. Pronoun agreement problems are mainly concerned with the singular or plural possessive pronouns that act as adjectives. To determine if that possessive pronoun should be singular or plural requires you to find and analyze the antecedent of the pronoun. To be able to do that, you have to know what an antecedent is. What is the definition of antecedent?

On which page is this information found?

PREDICTING

C56. In your own words, state how the antecedent of a pronoun determines whether you should choose the possessive pronoun with the singular or plural characteristic.

Textbook quotes and pages that confirm your answer.

C57. Knowing the definition of antecedent and how the antecedent allows you to choose the pronoun with the correct characteristic is fine. These are the preliminary steps in the process. The major problem, however, is determining <u>which</u> word is the pronoun's antecedent.

How do you go about finding the antecedent of a pronoun so that you can choose the correct singular or plural pronoun? You will be glad to know that the four step process you learned in subject/verb agreement, with only a modification of the fourth step, can also be used to solve a major part of this pronoun problem. (This last statement should indicate to you that the antecedent of the pronoun is, in most cases, the subject of the simple sentence.) Write the first three steps of the subject/verb agreement process here.

STEP ONE:

STEP TWO:

STEP THREE:

PREDICTING

C58. Don't forget Step Three requires you to be aware of those 18 rules collected in B104 to determine if the subject is singular or plural! But in the meantime, let's think about Step Four in a pronoun agreement situation. Based on your answers to C55 to C57, develop what you think would be the final step that will enable you to solve pronoun agreement problems.

STEP FOUR:

C59. Discuss your Step Four with the class. But before the class agrees on a final step, there is another aspect of pronoun agreement that you will be required to incorporate into the fourth step. This aspect deals with the gender of the antecedent, as illustrated in the following sentence.

The young lady finally gave (her, his, their) answer.

Your research into pronouns should have uncovered that pronouns divide not only into singular and plural, but also have masculine (his), feminine (her), and neuter (its) characteristics. How can the antecedent help solve this aspect of the pronoun choice?

ANALYZING

Textbook quotes and pages that confirm your answer.

C60. The pronoun choice is easy when the antecedent is clearly masculine or feminine. The following sentence illustrates a more difficult problem.

The student finally gave (his, her, its, their) answer.

What happens when, as in this sentence, an indefinite pronoun or a neutral noun such as *student* is used as the subject of the simple sentence and is therefore the antecedent of the pronoun? The singular/plural aspect of the problem is clear. But how do you determine if the pronoun should be masculine or feminine?

Textbook quotes and pages that confirm your answer.

C61. The answer to this problem is one that is currently in a state of transition. Traditionally, the pronoun *he* would be used to indicate both masculine and feminine when the gender of the antecedent was unclear. The women's rights movement pointed out the bias implied in this solution. The *his/her* or *his or her* combinations are a few of the suggested answers. You may have seen others. This is a good example of the versatility of the English language that this study guide has been emphasizing. What solution do you think is most useful?

Why?

DISCUSSING

C62. Discuss with your classmates what the final step of the pronoun agreement process should be. Then determine, as a class, the exact wording of the new and final step of the PRONOUN AGREEMENT STRATEGY. The wording should make the four-step pronoun agreement process efficient, clear, and useful. Note here the consensus of the class on the wording of step four.

STEP FOUR:

C63. Let's return to the sentence that initiated this discussion of pronoun agreement.

Every one of the students is going to (his, her, his/her, their) seat.

Using the four step pronoun agreement process, circle the correct pronoun in this sentence.

Why, in terms of antecedent characteristics, is *his/her* the correct pronoun choice?

C64. You will notice the practice sentences that follow are all simple sentences; that is, they contain one independent clause. (If you have any problems with the meanings of those terms, please consult your Personal Glossary in A4.) The use of simple sentences is deliberate because the pronoun agreement problems in complex sentences are more complex. (B57 indicated that these steps only solve a part, not all, of pronoun agreement problems.) But don't dismay, you will have the opportunity to investigate these more intricate pronoun agreement problems in Topic D.

In the meantime, you can sharpen your problem-solving skills in pronoun agreement on the following sentences. Perform each step of the four step pronoun agreement process to solve each of the practice sentences. To reinforce your knowledge and understanding of singular and plural subjects, you are also to indicate the singular/plural Rule number from B104.

		S/P Rule #		
s	p		A)	Everybody in the management division wants (his/her, their) way.
s	p		B)	The children always seem to get (his/her, their) way.
s	p		C)	A number of bridesmaids wore (her, their) own hand-made dress.
s	p		D)	The committee desires (its, their) solution to be recommended for adoption.
s	p		E)	<u>Walker, Jordan, and Post</u> insures (its, their) employees.
s	p		F)	The oxen can't seem to get out of (its, their) own way.
s	p		G)	A student wanting to study classics must make up (his, her, his/her, their) mind to do so at the end of (his, her, his/her, their) freshman year at college.
s	p		H)	All of the students brought (his/her, their) papers to the class.
s	p		I)	All of the class reported to (its, their) homeroom.
s	p		J)	Neither the boys from the first grade class nor that second grader found (his, their) notebook.
s	p		K)	Neither that second grader nor the boys from the first grade class found (his, their) books.
s	p		L)	Nobody washed (his or her, their) cup.

ANALYZING

C65. The following practice sentences contains at least one of the pronoun problems studied throughout this Topic. In order to reinforce an analytical, problem-solving approach to English grammar, perform the following steps:

1. Determine which FUNCTION STRATEGY and/or variation you will use;

2. Circle the correct pronoun; and

3. Explain your choice.

Be prepared to defend your answers in class.

a. You have been gardening much longer than (they, them).

THE FUNCTION STRATEGY IS:

EXPLANATION OF CHOICE:

b. Everyone making a large contribution will have (his, their) name on the cornerstone.

THE FUNCTION STRATEGY IS:

EXPLANATION OF CHOICE:

c. The waiter told Frank and (me, I) there were no more tables.

THE FUNCTION STRATEGY IS:

EXPLANATION OF CHOICE:

d. Two employees, you and (I, me), will represent the company next week.

THE FUNCTION STRATEGY IS:

EXPLANATION OF CHOICE:

e.   It's (I, me) whom you have to talk to!

THE FUNCTION STRATEGY IS:

EXPLANATION OF CHOICE:

f.   She bought (he, him) a gift.

THE FUNCTION STRATEGY IS:

EXPLANATION OF CHOICE:

C66. The sentences in the following paragraph do not have the pronoun choices given. Correct the pronoun errors, if any, which you find. Be prepared to defend your answers in class.

Everybody can now use their thinking skills to solve problems in English grammar. In fact, thinking skills can be used by we students in all our classes. We can classify, problem solve, compare definitions, and evaluate usefulness. The instructor doesn't have to tell we students what to do. We can do it by ourselves because we have good researching skills. Between you and I, it's a much more interesting way to learn.

```
. . . CHECK IT OUT, AGAIN! . . .
```

C67. Go back through the paragraph you wrote in C1 and determine if your sentences contain any pronoun agreement situations. If yes, use the four step PRONOUN AGREEMENT STRATEGY to determine if you had chosen the correct singular or plural possessive pronoun. Be prepared to place your sentence on the board and lead a class discussion.

PROOFREADING

C68. If your paragraph contains pronouns different from the ones analyzed in this Topic or used in ways not covered by this Topic, research the rules that cover the situation. Be prepared to instruct the class on the sentence containing the new pronoun or the new pronoun use.

ANALYZING A SENTENCE: PARTS OF SPEECH, CHARACTERISTICS, AND FUNCTIONS

C69. This is another exercise in labeling parts of speech, their characteristics and functions. Remember, these exercises integrate your learning; not only your learning about grammar but also your learning about using textbooks and dictionaries to solve problems.

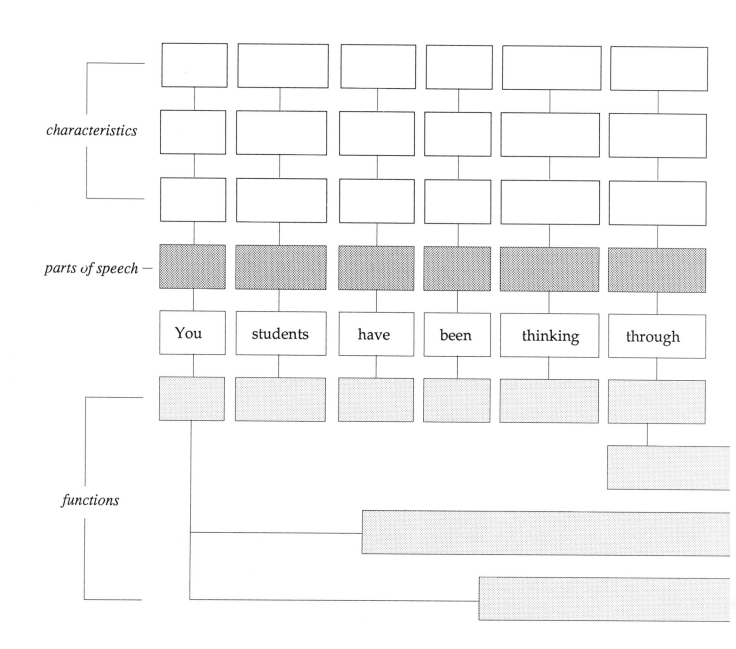

characteristics

parts of speech —

You | students | have | been | thinking | through

functions

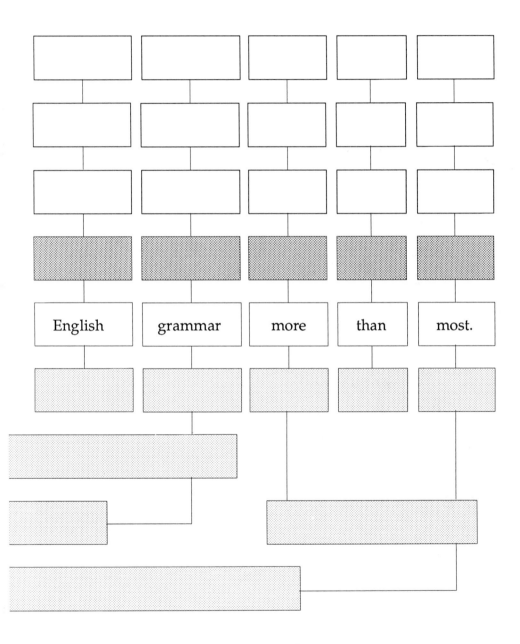

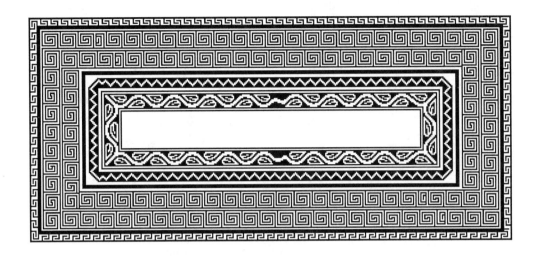

Topic D:
Synthesizing Subjects, Verbs, Clauses
And Sentences

You have, to this point, been asked to integrate (Topic A), analyze (Topic B), and think strategically about information (Topic C). Each topic demanded a different level of skill and knowledge. Now you will, in this Topic, learn to combine these skills and knowledge to develop an understanding and appreciation of sentence structure, the basic framework of written and oral communication.

You will be working with some familiar grammatical terms and concepts in this Topic. You have studied the different kinds of clauses and the types of sentences that can be created when you combine clauses. Now you will go deeper into these well-known areas. Use what you already know as a frame of reference, as a basis to build upon. You will also be working with familiar thinking and problem-solving skills. You have had much practice in using reference skills to locate information, in analyzing definitions and concepts, in developing strategies to

solve problems. Use them all as a basis for learning to synthesize information, to deepen your understanding. Learning to synthesize knowledge and information, to examine and think through questions are abilities of the highest level.

You are not asked as often as you were before to indicate how you found material or what your mind did to determine answers. The questions aren't asked because the instructor assumes you do this automatically at this point. If you have any problem with being aware of how your mind makes decisions, please take some time to study this. You can, at any time and any place in this Topic, ask yourself, "What steps did my mind take to answer this question?" Write out these steps so you can determine if there are any points in the process you want to examine and refine. You should be a sufficiently self-motivated learner at this point to want to be aware of your thinking.

```
┌─────────────────────────┐
│                         │
│    LET'S WRITE . . .    │
│                         │
└─────────────────────────┘
```

D1. Write a 100 word paragraph about a famous person or an experience that has influenced your life. Please triple space the paragraph.

```
┌──────────────────────────────────────────────┐
│                                              │
│   CLAUSES, THE ROOT OF THE SENTENCE          │
│                                              │
└──────────────────────────────────────────────┘
```

DEFINING

D2. Define a clause.

On which pages is this information found?

PROBLEM-SOLVING

D3. As you discovered from your definition of clause above, it is vital that you be able to find subjects and verbs in sentences. Write here the strategy you developed in Topic C to find subjects in sentences.

STEP ONE:

STEP TWO:

STEP THREE:

STEP FOUR:

STEP FIVE:

PROBLEM-SOLVING

D4. Since finding verbs is sometimes part of the strategy to find subjects, write a strategy to find verbs in a sentence.

STEP ONE:

STEP TWO:

STEP THREE:

STEP FOUR:

STEP FIVE:

PRACTICE

D5. <u>Subject and verb combinations</u> are the building blocks upon which all sentence analysis is based. They are the key to understanding clauses and sentences. It is, therefore, important that you know well the strategies necessary to find them.

APPLYING

The following sentences, taken from this study guide, were deliberately chosen because they are long and complex. They are not unlike sentences you might encounter in your other texts. These sentences are used to ensure your mastery of the vital task of finding subjects and verbs. Circle subjects and underline verbs in the following sentences.

a.   <u>Thinking Your Way Through English Grammar</u> concentrates on the

      English grammar component of the tapestry of written communica-

      tion.

b.   Grammar rules are broadly explored as an organized field of study

      so that the student may then meaningfully relate them to the larger

      field of personal communication.

c.   The student will learn valuable thinking skills that are transferable to

      learning content material in any other organized field of study.

d.   As you go through this course, make a conscious effort to be aware of

      the steps your mind goes through as it answers questions and solves

      problems.

e.   Since subject and verb combinations are the building blocks upon

      which all sentence structure is based, it is important that you know and

      can use the strategies necessary to find them.

f.   Circle subjects and underline verbs in the following sentences.

ANALYZING

D6. Using your paragraph from D1, circle each subject and underline each verb. Your instructor will indicate certain of your sentences to be placed on the board. Be prepared to lead the class in picking out subjects and verbs in these sentences.

> KINDS OF CLAUSES

DEFINING

D7. Name the two kinds of clauses and write the textbook definition of each.

1.

2.

On which pages is this information found?

COMPARING

D8. Compare the textbook definition you discovered for dependent (subordinate) clause with the following:

> A dependent clause is a group of words containing a subject and a verb combination and always starts with a subordinating conjunction or relative pronoun. (Both the latter terms are sometimes collectively referred to as *dependent clause signals*.)

Determine which definition is most useful to you and explain your choice.

D9. It is obvious that in order for you to fully understand the definition of dependent clause, you have to know and understand subordinating conjunctions and relative pronouns.

LISTING

Make a list of the subordinating conjunctions that can introduce subordinate clauses.

On which pages is this information found?

Put an asterisk next to those subordinating conjunctions that can function as other parts of speech.

(Review C13-C15 for the pronoun problem caused by the subordinating conjunction *since* when it functions as a preposition.)

D10. Make a list of the relative pronouns that introduce subordinate clauses. LISTING

On which pages is this information found?

Put an asterisk next to those relative pronouns that can function as other parts of speech.

D11. Write two examples of a dependent clause; use a different subordinate conjunction in each. Write two more examples of a dependent clause; use a different relative pronoun in each. Be prepared to defend your examples in class. *WRITING EXAMPLES*

1.

2.

3.

4.

D12. Compare the textbook definition of independent (sometimes referred to as main) clause you discovered in D7 with the following: *COMPARING*

An independent clause is a group of words that contains a subject and verb combination and does NOT start with a subordinating conjunction or relative pronoun.

Determine which definition is most useful to you and explain your choice. *DECIDING*

D13. Write three examples of independent clauses. Be prepared to defend your examples in class. *WRITING EXAMPLES*

1.

2.

3.

ANALYZING

D14. Using your paragraph from D1, put parentheses around each clause and label each clause as either dependent or independent. Your instructor will indicate certain of your sentences to be placed on the board. Be prepared to lead the class in a discussion in the labeling of clauses in your sentences.

SYNTHESIZING

D15. Let's put all this knowledge together in a structured overview. Place the following words in the appropriate boxes so that they express the proper relationship among the terms. (If you have any difficulty with these instructions, see A28 for more details.)

Subject, Verb, Clause, Independent Clause, Subordinating Conjunction, Subject, Verb, Dependent Clause, Relative Pronoun

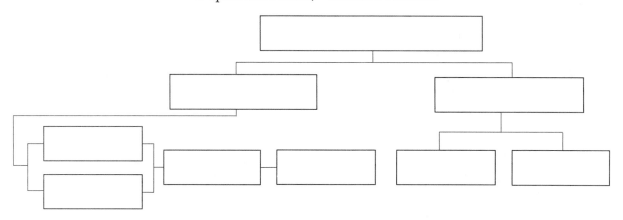

KINDS OF SENTENCES

DEFINING

D16. Define a simple sentence.

CREATING

D17. If your text defines a simple sentence without using the term independent clause, write a definition which incorporates that term. Be prepared to defend your definition.

DEFINING

D18. Define a compound sentence.

On which pages is this information found?

D19. If your text defines a compound sentence without using the term independent clause, write a definition using that term. Be prepared to defend your definition.

D20. It is time to integrate your knowledge of the two sentence types (simple and compound sentences) with two other terms: compound subjects and compound verbs. Define:

COMPOUND SUBJECT

COMPOUND VERB (PREDICATE)

On which pages is this information found?

D21. Based on your understanding of the definitions of clause, independent clause, simple sentence, compound sentence, compound subject, and compound verb, answer the following questions and be prepared to defend your answers.

A. Can a simple sentence have a compound subject?
    Explain your reasoning.

    Write a simple sentence that contains a compound subject.

B. Can a simple sentence have a compound verb?
    Explain your reasoning.

    Write a simple sentence that contains a compound verb.

C. Can a simple sentence have a compound subject and a
    compound verb?
    Explain your reasoning.

    Write a simple sentence that contains a compound subject and a
    compound verb.

D. If a simple sentence can have a compound subject and a compound
    verb, why isn't it called a compound sentence?

E.   Does a compound sentence have to have a compound subject? Explain.

F.   Can a compound sentence have a compound subject and/or a compound verb?
Explain your reasoning.

EXPLAINING

D22. Is the following sentence simple or compound?

Jack and Jill frolicked and cavorted on a steep and treacherous incline.

Explain your reasoning.

> ANALYZE A SENTENCE: PARTS OF SPEECH,
> CHARACTERISTICS, AND FUNCTIONS

D23. Let's use this newly developed knowledge to analyze the sentence below by labeling the part of speech, the characteristics, and the function of each word in the sentence.

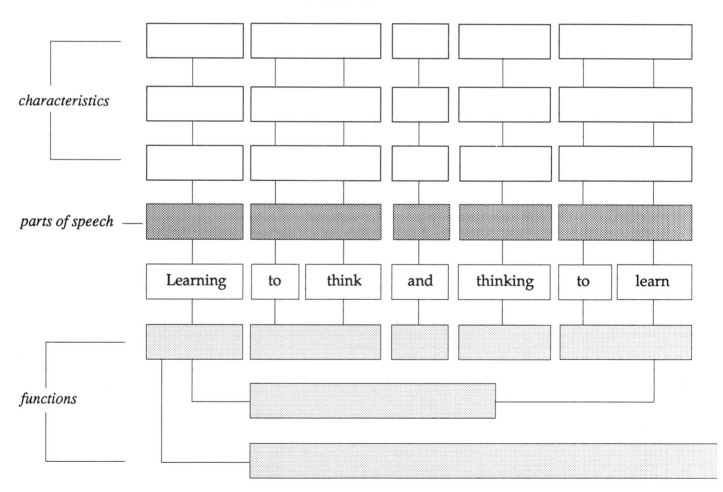

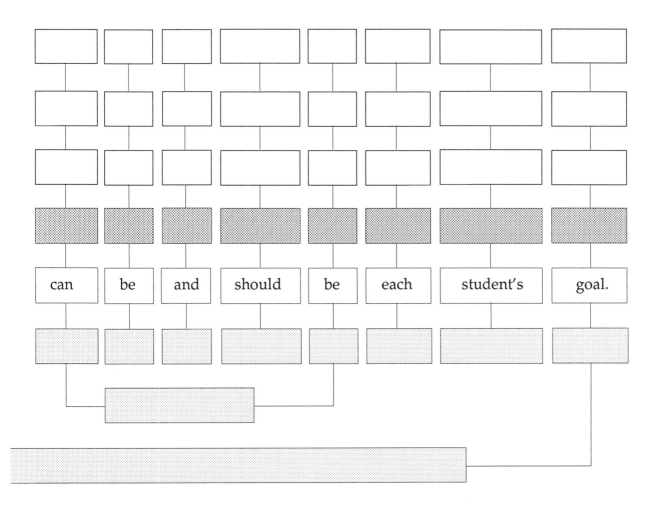

can	be	and	should	be	each	student's	goal.

D24. How can the definitions of clauses and simple and compound sentences be modified to incorporate the problem of compound subjects and verbs?

CLAUSE

SIMPLE SENTENCE

COMPOUND SENTENCE

PROBLEM-SOLVING

D25. What strategy will you use to ensure you do not confuse a compound subject and/or verb in a simple sentence with a compound sentence?

PRACTICE

APPLYING

D26. The practice sentences in D5 contained examples of both simple and compound subjects and verbs. Go back to the sentences in D5 and indicate above each subject and verb whether it is simple or compound. Connect compound words/functions with a line.

RESEARCHING

D27. One final aspect of compound sentences is how they can be punctuated. Find in your text three ways, other than separating the independent clauses with a period, that can be used to punctuate compound sentences.

1.

2.

3.

On which pages is this information found?

LISTING

D28. Name the two different kinds of conjunctions used to separate the independent clauses in a compound sentence and give some examples.

                                        Examples
1.

2.

On which pages is this information found?

D29. Write three of your own compound sentences. Each sentence should use a different punctuation method. Be prepared to place these sentences on the board and conduct the class in an analysis of the sentences.

1.

2.

3.

D30. Define a complex sentence.

On which pages is this information found?

D31. You should have discovered that subject verb combinations are the key to finding clauses and thereby determining if sentences are simple, compound, or complex. But you know from Topic B that words and phrases may come between a subject and a verb.

In complex sentences, whole clauses may come between a subject and its verb in the independent clause! This makes subject verb combinations even more interesting. Circle the subject and underline the verbs in the following sentences. Use a line to connect each subject with its verb. Here is an example:

Subordinate (clauses) (which) come between subject and verb require careful analysis.

a. The car that Sheila bought is practical.

b. The car that I buy, when my finances permit, will also have to be practical.

c. The car that the company where I work must buy, on the other hand,

will have to be very big and luxurious.

D32. How do you punctuate complex sentences?

On which pages is this information found?

D33. Define a compound/complex sentence.

D34. Let's add to the structured overview started in D15. Fill in the words in the boxes below as they appeared in D15. Then draw lines to the four boxed sentence types to indicate visually the relationships between these terms.

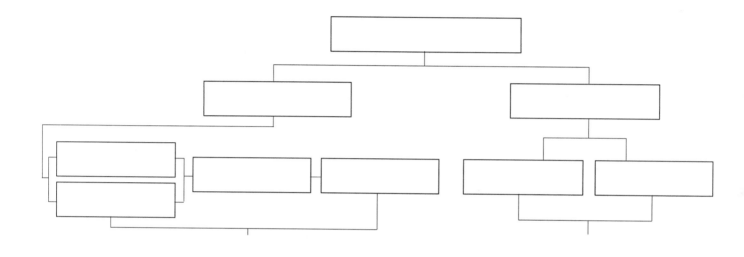

| complex sentence | comp./compl. sent. | compound sent. | simple sentence |

PRACTICE

D35. Practice your understanding and application of many of the terms you've examined so far in the sentences below: (1) Circle the subject(s) and underline the verb(s). (2) Label whether the subjects and/or verbs are compound or simple. (3) Put parenthesis around each clause and label each clause as independent or dependent. (4) Insert the proper punctuation. (5) In the margin, label the sentence as simple, compound or complex. Be able to defend each of your decisions.

Sentence Type

    a.   Terri and Frank went to the store.

b.   Terri and Frank went to the store and bought bread.

c.   Terri and Frank went to the store and they bought bread.

d.   Terri and Frank went to the store they bought bread.

e.   Terri and Frank went to the store however they forgot to buy bread.

f.   When Terri and Frank went to the store they bought bread.

g.   Terri and Frank bought bread when they went to the store.

h.   When Terri and Frank went to the store they bought bread for they needed to make sandwiches for the picnic.

```
... CHECK IT OUT, AGAIN ...
```

D36. Go back to your paragraph from D1. Label each sentence as one of the three sentence types. Determine if you have properly punctuated them. Your instructor will indicate certain of your sentences to be placed on the board. Be prepared to lead the class in a discussion of these sentences.

PROOFREADING

D37. Let's use this knowledge to analyze a rather complicated sentence. Label the part of speech, the characteristics, and the function of each word as indicated in the structured overview below.

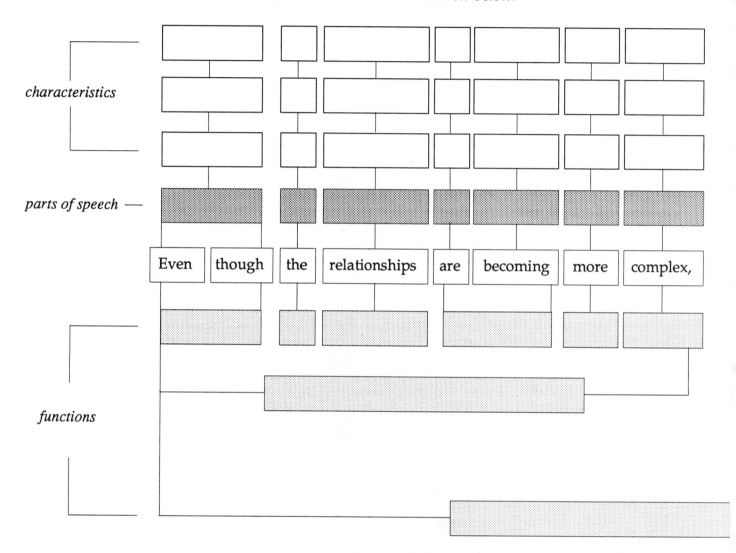

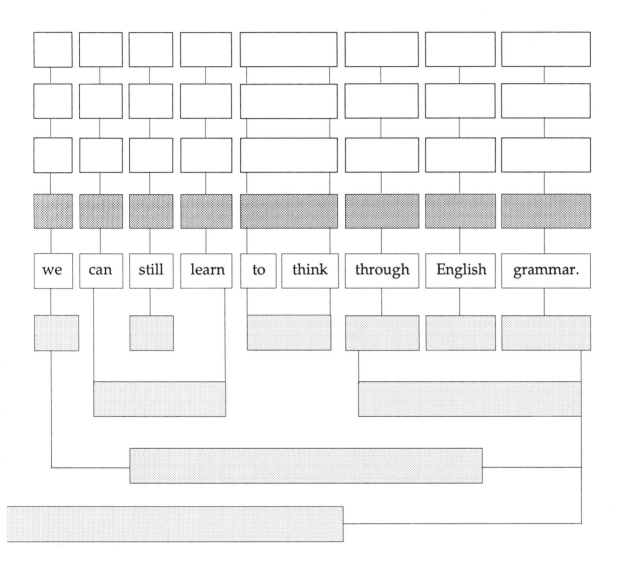

we | can | still | learn | to | think | through | English | grammar.

D38. A reason for understanding the structure of the sentence is so that you can recognize the difference between complete sentences and fragments in your writing. Complete sentences promote clear and effective communication; fragments do not. No one may ask you in five years whether you know the difference between a compound sentence and a complex sentence, but the analysis you just went through will prepare you to know whether you have written complete sentences in your own reports and letters.

DEFINING

In question D12, a definition of independent clause was suggested. Use that definition to define a sentence.

SENTENCE:

What does your text say a fragment is?

On which pages is this information found?

PROBLEM-SOLVING

D39. From your definition of a sentence, what three elements will you look for to determine if you have written a fragment or a sentence?

I will look for:

1.

2.

3.

DISCUSSING

D40. Discuss your three elements in class and attempt to agree as a class on the three elements. Note here any revisions and/or important points made during the discussion.

D41. Using your three element strategy, determine if the following are sentences or fragments by writing your choice in the margin. The reason for your choice must include reference to the presence or absence of the appropriate element.

Fragment or Sentence

a.   The study guide on the desk.

REASON:

b.   The study guide that I used.

REASON:

c.   On the desk.

REASON:

d.   The study guide on the desk that I used.

REASON:

e.   The study guide that I used for my English grammar courses in my Freshman and Sophomore years.

REASON:

f.   Since I used that study guide.

REASON:

g.   Read that study guide!

REASON:

h.   Since using that study guide.

REASON:

i.   The class using the study guide.

REASON:

j.   The classes using the study guide did very well in their English composition courses.

REASON:

┌─────────────────────────────────┐
│   . . . CHECK IT OUT AGAIN! . . .   │
└─────────────────────────────────┘

PROOFREADING

D42. Go back through your paragraph in D1 and (1) determine if there are any fragments, (2) indicate what makes them a fragment, and (3) correct the error. Your instructor will indicate certain of your sentences to be placed on the board. Be prepared to lead the class in a discussion of these sentences.

┌─────────────────────────────────┐
│   DEPENDENT CLAUSES: A SYNTHESIS   │
└─────────────────────────────────┘

D43. You are now going to investigate in more detail the subordinate or dependent clause. This analysis ties together many of the threads that were woven throughout this entire text.

You have seen that individual words are parts of speech and that part of speech many times depends on how the word functions in a sentence. But can a group of words, like a clause, function as a part of speech?

FINDING PROOF

What is your proof?

On which pages is this information found?

LISTING

D44. A dependent clause can function as three parts of speech. Name them.

On which pages is this information found?

D45. You discovered in D9 and D10 that subordinating conjunctions and relative pronouns introduce dependent clauses. Let's get more precise. Determine which kinds of clause the subordinate conjunction and the relative pronoun introduce.

SUBORDINATING CONJUNCTION INTRODUCES:

RELATIVE PRONOUN INTRODUCES:

On which pages is this information found?

D46. The sentences below contain clauses that act as each of these three parts of speech. (1) Underline the subordinate clause, (2) label each dependent clause as one of the parts of speech, (3) give the reasons for your answer, and (4) if the clause functions as a noun, indicate the function the noun clause performs; if an adverb or adjective clause, give the word it modifies.

a.   What the candidate said yesterday was changed today.

PART OF SPEECH OF THE DEPENDENT CLAUSE:

REASON FOR YOUR CHOICE:

WORD MODIFIED OR FUNCTION PERFORMED:

b.   When the candidate made his statement yesterday, he was unaware of the current conditions.

PART OF SPEECH OF THE DEPENDENT CLAUSE:

REASON FOR YOUR CHOICE:

WORD MODIFIED OR FUNCTION PERFORMED:

c.   The candidate's statement, which was made yesterday, had overlooked current conditions.

PART OF SPEECH OF THE DEPENDENT CLAUSE:

REASON FOR YOUR CHOICE:

WORD MODIFIED OR FUNCTION PERFORMED:

D47. The adjective clause is the one that creates problems of pronoun form, omitted words, dual functions, subject/verb agreement, pronoun reference, and punctuation. These are topics that you have followed throughout this study guide. You will need all your reference skills and strategy resources to synthesize your knowledge to put the final threads of this grammar tapestry together.

Since the relative pronouns that introduce the adjective dependent clause are such important elements of the following analysis, rewrite the relative pronouns from D10 here.

THE ADJECTIVE CLAUSE
AND PRONOUN FORM

RESEARCHING

D48. Do you remember in Topics B and C that the function a personal pronoun performs determines whether you would use the nominative or objective characteristics of the pronoun? Well, relative pronouns also have different forms, like *who*, *which*, or *that*. However, choosing the correct relative pronoun does not always depend on the function the pronoun is performing since these three relative pronouns often function as the subject of the dependent clause. There are other considerations that determine which to use. Use your text to determine when to use *who*, *which*, and *that*.

On which pages is this information found?

RESEARCHING

D49. Choosing between *who* and *whom*, on the other hand, does depend on the function the word is performing in the clause. When do you use *who* and when do you use *whom*?

On which pages is this information found?

COMPARING

D50. Compare your text's explanation of when to use *who* and *whom* with the following:

> Isolate the dependent clause that is started by *who* or *whom*. Determine if that dependent clause has a subject other than the relative pronoun. If the dependent clause does not have a subject, then the correct relative choice is *who*. If the dependent clause already has a subject other than the relative pronoun, then the correct relative pronoun choice is *whom*.

D51. Based on your research for the last two questions, choose the correct relative pronoun in the following sentences and give the reasons for your choices.

a. The person (which, that, who, whom) is wearing the red shirt placed first in the competition.

REASON:

b. The car (which, that, who, whom) has the red side trim placed first in the race.

REASON:

c. The dog (which, that, who, whom) is wearing the red collar placed first in the competition.

REASON:

d. The person (which, that, who, whom) you noticed in the red shirt won the race.

REASON:


```
┌─────────────────────────────────┐
│  THE ADJECTIVE CLAUSE           │
│  AND IMPLIED WORDS              │
└─────────────────────────────────┘
```

D52. You have reviewed omitted or implied words two previous times in this study guide. Can you name the two situations?

1.

2.

D53. The following sentence contains a dependent clause. Can you pick it out?

The computer I buy will have many graphic capabilities.

What is the dependent word signal?

On which pages of your text do you find support for your conclusion?

D54. The following sentences contain implied words involving the three situations discussed in the last two questions. Indicate the implied words or word and state its function.

a.   Stop!

IMPLIED WORD AND ITS FUNCTION:

b.   The essay he wrote earned him an A.

IMPLIED WORD AND ITS FUNCTION:

c.   Susan likes John better than him.

IMPLIED WORD AND ITS FUNCTION:

D55. Let's put a name to the two dependent clauses represented by the sentences "b" and "c" in D54. Search your text for the name of the type of clause that omits some of its words.

On which pages is this information found?

Why are these words omitted?

> THE ADJECTIVE CLAUSE AND WORDS
> PERFORMING DUAL FUNCTIONS

D56. Words performing dual functions have not been discussed so far in this study guide. The closest you came to this concept was the word *her* in the sentence "Aunt Mildred feeds her dog biscuits." You discovered *her* could function either as an indirect object or a possessive pronoun modifying dog.

In the following complex sentence, one word performs two functions at the same time. It is not an "either or" situation; the word <u>does</u> perform two functions at the same time.

Heather is one of those students who (is, are) always early to class.

(1) Circle the subject and underline the verb in each clause. (2) Place brackets around the relative pronoun (or dependent word signal as it is sometimes called). (3) Indicate which clause is independent and which is dependent.

D57. Name the word that performs two functions and name the two functions.

D58. Discuss any problems you think might arise because of this situation.

┌─────────────────────────────────────┐
│ THE ADJECTIVE CLAUSE AND   │
│ SUBJECT/VERB AREEMENT   │
└─────────────────────────────────────┘

D59. Subject/verb agreement was a major grammatical concept that you investigated in depth in this study guide in Topic B. You will now synthesize the skills and strategies developed there with strategies developed in the pronoun reference section of Topic C.

The sentence you will explore is taken from D56. Try to use the four step subject/verb agreement process developed in Topic B to pick the correct verb in the following sentence.   *PREDICTING*

      Heather is one of those students who (is, are) always early to class.

What difficulties did you have using the four step subject/verb agreement process from Topic B in this situation?

D60. What word did you circle as the subject of the verb in question?   *EXPLAINING*

Is that subject singular or plural?

Explain your choice.

D61. You can see, again, that it is determining whether the subject is singular or plural that is the difficult part of subject/verb agreement problems. When the subject of the dependent clause is *who*, you can't tell whether *who* is singular or plural.

What step from your pronoun reference strategy in Topic C do you think you can use to determine whether *who* in the above sentence is singular or plural?   *REMEMBERING*

PREDICTING	D62. If you answered that you have to find the antecedent of *who*, you would be correct. But the next problem is to determine what word is the antecedent. Referring back to the sentence that started this discussion —

Heather is one of those students who (is, are) always early to class.

— what might you predict to be the antecedent of *who*?

RESEARCHING	There seems to be three choices for the antecedent of *who*: it could be *Heather, one,* or *students*. Use your text to determine which of the three words is the proper antecedent and write the rule for this situation here.

COMPARING	D63. Compare your predicted answer and the text's answer. Discuss the problem in class and note important points from the class discussion.

PROBLEM-SOLVING	D64. Create a subject/verb agreement strategy for verb choices in relative clauses. (If you need more than five steps, write the additional steps in the margins.)

STEP ONE:

STEP TWO:

STEP THREE:

STEP FOUR:

STEP FIVE:

APPLYING	D65. Perform all the steps of your subject/verb agreement strategy for relative clauses to determine the correct verb in the sentence that started this discussion:

Heather is one of those students who (is, are) always early to class.

Be prepared to defend your answer.

D66. Choosing the correct verb in the sentence in D65 is based in part on the premise that clear writing demands that a pronoun be located as closely as possible to its antecedent.

PREDICTING

This rule—that a pronoun's antecedent is usually the immediately preceding noun or pronoun— is, unfortunately, not applicable to every situation. What do you think is the antecedent of the relative pronoun in the following sentence?

> Heather is the only one of the students who (is, are) early to class.

RESEARCHING

D67. Find what your textbook indicates is the rule that covers this situation.

On which pages is this information found?

DISCUSSING

D68. Here's another example of an exception:

> The men of the third brigade who are here will continue the exercise.

Discuss as a class how you will go about determining whether the noun or pronoun immediately preceding the relative pronouns *who*, *which*, or *that* is the antecedent or not.

APPLYING

D69. Perform each step in your subject/verb agreement strategy for verbs in independent and relative clauses to choose the correct verb in the following sentences. (Besides circling subjects and putting an "s" or "p" in the margin, place an "a" over the word you determine is the antecedent of the relative pronoun.)

a. The cars which (is, are) in the driveway are not mine!

b. The cars in the driveway which (is, are) next to the house are not mine!

c. The cars that he (owns, own) are in the driveway.

d. That is the car which (is, are) mine.

e. That old station wagon is one of the cars that (has, have)

   been dependable for me.

f. That old station wagon is the only one of the cars that (has, have)

   survived all the drivers in the family.

g. The only cars that I ever owned (was, were) bought from the

   same dealer!

h. Only one of the cars that (was, were) bought from that dealer was

   a lemon.

D70. Analyze the sentence below in the usual manner: label the part of
speech, the characteristics, and the functions of each word as indicated in the
structured overview.

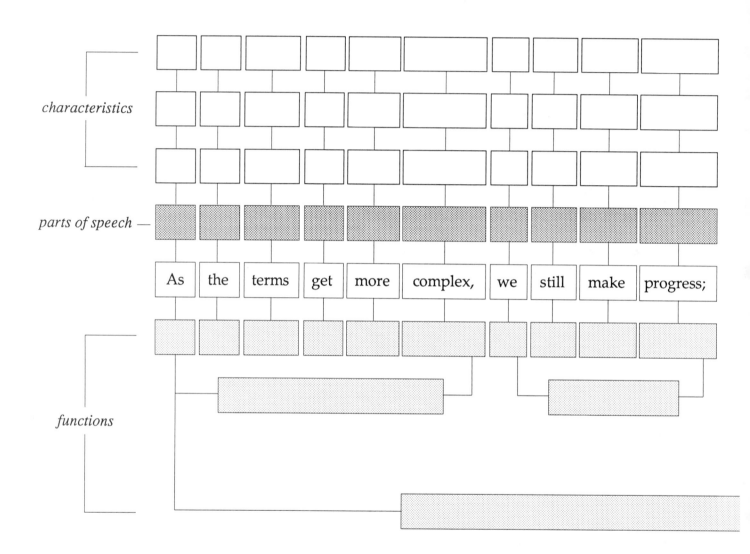

characteristics

parts of speech —

As | the | terms | get | more | complex, | we | still | make | progress;

functions

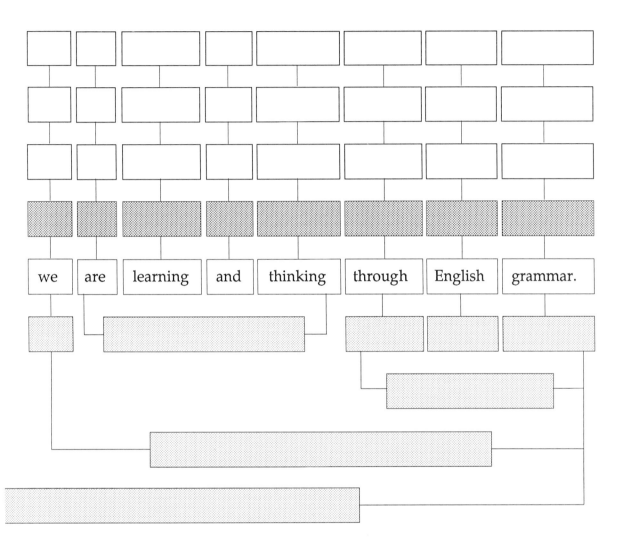

we | are | learning | and | thinking | through | English | grammar.

ANALYZING

D71. In the following sentences, circle the correct word for each of the choices given and state the reason for your choice.

A. The Grahams, (who, which, whom, that)¹ (collects, collect)² quilts, also (refinishes, refinish)³ antique furniture.

1. REASON:

2. REASON:

3. REASON:

B. One of the instructors (who, which, whom, that)¹ (teaches, teach)² in the computer lab (comes, come)³ directly from work experience in industry.

1. REASON:

2. REASON:

3. REASON:

C. Wonder Cream is the only one of the hand cleaning products (who, which, whom, that)¹ (deserves, deserve)² to be reordered.

1. REASON:

2. REASON:

D.   Wonder Cream is one of the hand cleaning products

                             1.   2.

(who, which, whom, that) (deserves, deserve) to be reordered.

1.   REASON:

2.   REASON:

┌─────────────────────────────────────┐
│   │
│   . . . CHECK IT OUT, AGAIN . . .   │
│   │
└─────────────────────────────────────┘

D72. Go back through the paragraph you wrote in D1 and do the following: *APPLYING*

(1)   Place brackets around those sentences in which a dependent clause functions as a noun.

(2)   Circle the sentences which uses *who* or *whom* as a relative pronoun.

(3)   Place a check mark in front of those sentences which have implied relative pronouns.

(4)   Circle every relative pronoun that also acts as the subject of a dependent clause.

(5)   Place an "a" over antecedents of relative pronouns.

Your instructor will indicate certain of your sentences to be placed on the board for class discussion. Be prepared to defend your analysis.

┌──────────────────────────────┐
│   ADJECTIVE CLAUSES AND   │
│   PRONOUN REFERENCE   │
└──────────────────────────────┘

D73. The adjective clause can also contain a pronoun reference problem as illustrated in the following sentence:

Heather is one of those students who are always the first in (her, their) seats.

The pronoun agreement rule that you had developed in Topic C involved   *PREDICTING*
a simple sentence. (See C51 through C65 for your rule.) Try to use your pronoun agreement strategy from Topic C to pick the correct pronoun in the above sentence.

What difficulties did you have using your pronoun reference strategy in this sentence?

D74. To be able to answer the questions in D73, you had to determine the antecedent for the pronoun. What word did you determine to be the antecedent of the pronoun in question?

What function does the antecedent of the pronoun perform in this sentence?

What problem did you have in determining whether the antecedent of the pronoun is singular or plural?

REMEMBERING

D75. Notice the spiral you are in! To determine whether the pronoun's antecedent is singular or plural means you have to find the antecedent of the antecedent! How will you determine the antecedent of the antecedent?

APPLYING

D76. Use this strategy to determine the correct pronoun in the sentence that started this discussion:

Heather is one of those students who are always the first in (her, their) seats.

Be prepared to defend your answer.

PRACTICE

EXPLAINING

D77. Circle the correct words for each of the choices given in the following sentences and state the reason for your choice.

1.
A.   Everybody in both divisions (who, which, that, whom)
            2.   3.   4.
      (attends, attend) the meetings (wants, want) (his/her, their) way.

1.   REASON:

2.   REASON:

3.   REASON:

4.   REASON:

B. The children (who, which, that, whom)¹ Maggie (care, cares)² for always
   (seems, seem)³ to get in (his, her, their)⁴ way.

1. REASON:

2. REASON:

3. REASON:

4. REASON:

C. The committee (who, which, that, whom)¹ (desires, desire)² (its, their)³
   solution to be recommended for adoption (have, has)⁴ taken full page
   advertisements in the local paper in support of (its, their)⁵ position.

1. REASON:

2. REASON:

3. REASON:

4. REASON:

5. REASON:

D. Frank is the only one of the employees (who, which, that, whom) ¹
(works, work) ² for <u>Walker, Jordan, and Post</u> (who, which, that, whom) ³
(has, have) ⁴ (his, their, its) ⁵ own company car.

1. REASON:

2. REASON:

3. REASON:

4. REASON:

5. REASON:

E. The oxen (who, which, that, whom) ¹ (belongs, belong) ² to farmer Jones
can't seem to get out of (its, their) ³ own way.

1. REASON:

2. REASON:

3. REASON:

F. All members of the class (who, which, that, whom) ¹ reported to
(its, their) ² homeroom for the extra credit assignment (was, were) ³
praised for (its, their) ⁴ punctuality.

1. REASON:

2. REASON:

3. REASON:

4. REASON:

G. Neither the boys from the first grade class nor that second grader
              1.   2.   3.
    (who, which, that, whom) lost (his, their) notebook (was, were) tardy.

1. REASON:

2. REASON:

3. REASON:

RESTRICTIVE AND NONRESTRICTIVE
ADJECTIVE CLAUSES AND THE COMMA

D78. The final thread that has to be placed in the adjective clause tapestry concerns punctuation: when to use, and when not to use, commas around the adjective clause.

The situation arises out of the function of this clause as an adjective; that is, the fact that this clause often modifies the noun which precedes it.

Here are two sentences that illustrate the situation.

A. The gentleman who owns the red convertible went into the store.

B. Tony who owns the red convertible went into the store.

In one of those sentences, commas should be placed around the dependent clause *who owns the red convertible*, and in the other sentence, no commas are required around the very same clause.

Without reference to your text, can you determine which sentence requires commas around the adjective clause; explain your reasoning.

PREDICTING

Sentence _____ requires commas and sentence _____ does not require commas.

EXPLANATION:

D79. Let's find out how accurate you were in your prediction. Find the definition of a restrictive clause in your text and write it here.

RESEARCHING

On which pages is this information found?

Find the definition of a nonrestrictive clause in your text and write it here.

On which pages is this information found?

EXPLAINING

D80. Based on these two definitions, explain in your own words why there should be commas around the relative clause in sentence B:

Tony, who owns the red convertible, went into the store.

D81. Based on these two definitions, explain in your own words why there should not be commas around the relative clause in sentence A:

The gentleman who owns the red convertible went into the store.

> PRACTICE

ANALYZING

D82. Place commas around the relative clauses in the following sentences where necessary. Explain your decision.

A. The friends with whom I went hiking are planning some more adventures.

REASON:

B. We visited Shining Rock Wilderness area which is located off the Blue Ridge Parkway in North Carolina and plan to hike there again.

REASON:

C. The most exciting hike that we took was to climb down to the Green River Narrows.

REASON:

D.   The Narrows which is surrounded by mountains has no road access and requires a difficult descent and arduous ascent.

REASON:

┌───┐
│   │
│   . . . CHECK IT OUT ONE LAST TIME!   │
│   │
└───┘

D83. Using the paragraph you wrote in D1, label your relative clauses (if any) as either restrictive or nonrestrictive and determine if you had the correct punctuation. Your instructor will indicate certain of your sentences to be placed on the board. Be prepared to lead the class in an analysis of these sentences.

PROOFREADING

┌─────────────────────────────┐
│   │
│   MORE PRACTICE   │
│   │
└─────────────────────────────┘

D84. The sentences in the following paragraph do not highlight possible grammatical errors by offering you choices. The analysis you have to do here corresponds more closely to the analysis you have to perform on your own writing. Correct the errors, if any, which you find. Be prepared to defend your corrections in class.

APPLYING

When you started this class. You might have been skeptical about learning English grammar by doing your own research. You and your classmates have made an extensive examination of your textbook and the dictionary. These "learning how to learn" skills will help you in other courses in school, and can help you on the job as well. Those of you that did all the research required will benefit the most, you are now able to answer your own questions about your own writing. Researching information about English grammar which is a powerful way to learn prepares you to research changes in job and work technology in the future. Are you one of those students who is confident of his ability to handle the changes which is sure to come?

D85. Analyze the sentence below by labeling the part of speech, the characteristics, and the function of each word.

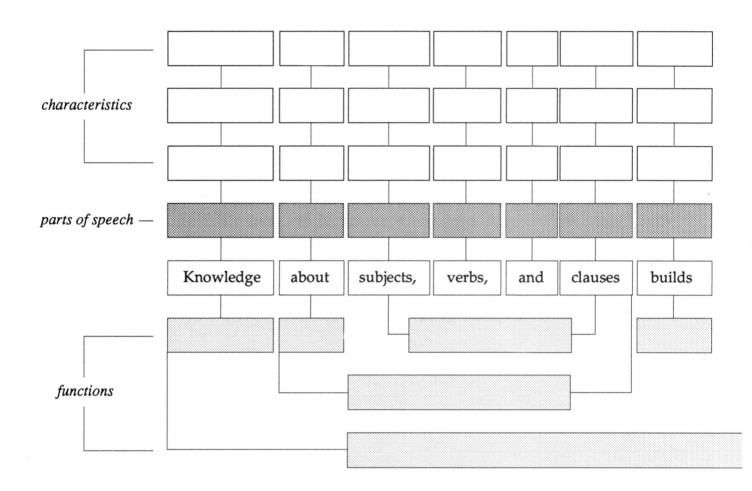

characteristics

parts of speech —

| Knowledge | about | subjects, | verbs, | and | clauses | builds |

functions

Do you now appreciate how part of speech is often determined by the function a word performs in a sentence, how characteristics of words are important in determining agreement problems, and how function determines pronoun form? Do you also appreciate why it is important to have the tools to analyze a sentence using this structured overview approach to keep the interrelationship of parts of speech, characteristics, and functions in a useable perspective?

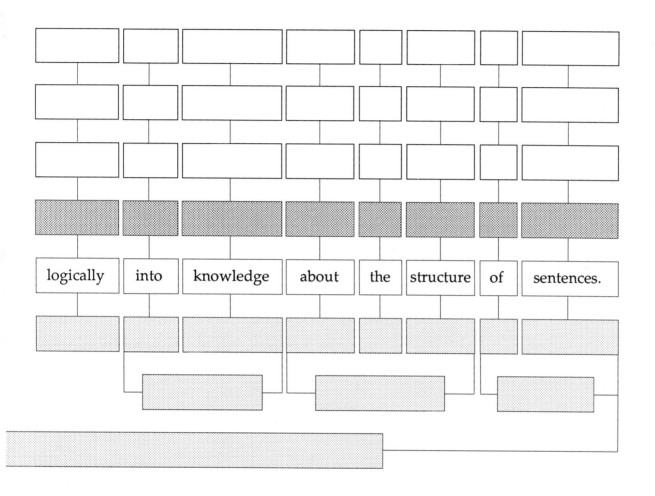

logically into knowledge about the structure of sentences.

TOPIC E:
EVALUATING COMPLEX RELATIONSHIPS: THE ANALOGY

Integrating the vocabulary of grammar, which you experienced in Topic A, is a basic component of the learning strategies explored in this course. There, relationships among English grammatical terms were examined through labeling, categorization, structured overviews, and classification. Topics B, C, and D focused on the understanding of terms to analyze specific grammatical problem areas.

In Topic E, you will have the opportunity to further improve your understanding of the relationships of these words as you perfect your tapestry of English grammar. You will refine your understanding through analogies.

Analogies are extremely powerful tools for learning the relationships of terms, concepts, and ideas. All the careful and precise thinking that you have developed with your research, predictions, strategies, analysis, and evaluations will be called upon as you work to solve and to create your own analogies.

All the careful and precise thinking that you have developed concerning grammatical terms will also be called upon. Analogies are the final thread in this English grammar tapestry. They are the finishing touch in which your expertise in thinking strategies and knowledge merge. They are the test by which you determine if the knowledge you have accumulated and the strategies you have developed will hang together to form a coherent whole.

This Topic has an added bonus. The strategies you develop to solve these grammatical analogies can be used to solve the analogies you will find in a variety of standard tests, including I.Q. tests and college and professional school entrance exams. Learn the process well here and transfer it when required to other situations.

E1. The analogy is a powerful technique for vocabulary building. The analogy forces you to explore a wide range of possible relationships between pairs of words. Sometimes the relationship is between the various definitions of words, other times the words' connotation, and still others their parts of speech. The list of possible relationships is endless. The solution is even more complicated because the relationship between the first set of words must be the very same relationship as between the second set of words.

Here are some steps to help you think through an analogy.

READING ANALOGIES: Analogies are presented as two pairs of words which are connected by symbols " : " and " :: ."

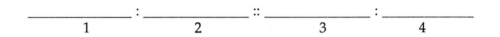

_____ : _____ :: _____ : _____
     1   2   3   4

The ":" symbol means *is related to*, and the "::" symbol means *in the same way as*. In other words, Word 1 *is related to* Word 2 *in the same way as* Word 3 *is related to* Word 4.

(A shortened version of this reads: Word 1 *is to* Word 2 *as* Word 3 *is to* Word 4 .)

One version of an analogy problem might look like this:

possessive : pronoun :: present tense : __?__

For purposes of illustration and instruction, the analogies in this book will look like this:

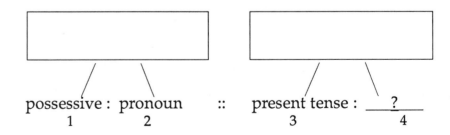

possessive : pronoun   ::   present tense : __?__
    1   2   3   4

The next four paragraphs model a step-by-step process for the solution of this form of analogy.

THE PROCESS FOR SOLUTION

STEP ONE. To solve this form of analogy, you are to find the relationship between Word 1 and Word 2 and write the relationship in the box provided above Word 1 and Word 2. Since *possessive* (Word 1) <u>is a type of</u> *pronoun* (Word 2), place that relationship in the first box.

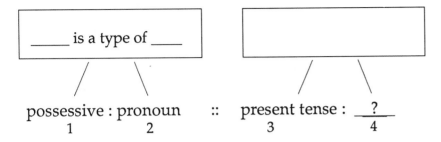

STEP TWO. This relationship between Word 1 and Word 2 is then rewritten in the space provided above Word 3 and Word 4.

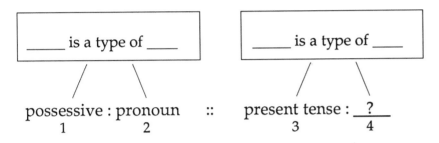

STEP THREE. Determine what *present tense* is a type of. Since *present tense* is a type of verb, then a possible correct answer is *verb*.

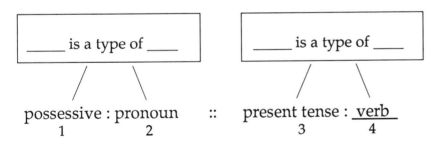

STEP FOUR. If the wording of the relationship expressed for Word 3 and Word 4 is altered in any way from the wording which expresses the relationship between Word 1 and Word 2, then the analogy is not correct. You must either change Word 4 or the relationship sentence or both. You will know that you have chosen the correct term for Word 4 when the relationship sentence for both sets of terms has the exact same wording.

THE RELATIONSHIP SENTENCE: The relationship in the boxes above each pair of words is sometimes called the relationship sentence. This sentence, as you can see, is exactly the same for both pairs of words. The relationship sentence is the key to ensuring that the analogy has been correctly solved.

There are an infinite number of relationship sentences. Here is a small sampling of the kinds of relationships that analogies using grammatical terms explore:

_____ is the same part of speech as _____
_____ is an example of _____
_____ is opposite of _____
_____ modifies _____

PRACTICE ANALOGIES

APPLYING

E2. Using the steps outlined above, complete the following analogies.

A.

plural : noun   ::   objective : _____

B.

interrogative : pronoun   ::   interrogative : _____

C.

adjective : noun   ::   adverb : _____

D.

very : quite   ::   slowly : _____

E.

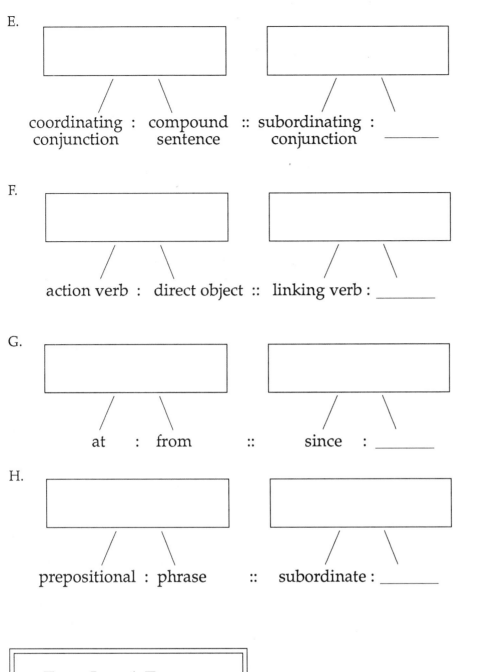

coordinating : compound :: subordinating :
conjunction   sentence   conjunction   ———

F.

action verb : direct object :: linking verb : _____

G.

at : from :: since : _____

H.

prepositional : phrase :: subordinate : _____

THINK LIKE A TEACHER

CREATING

E3. Now it is your turn. Create three analogies in the same form as those presented in E2. The first analogy should contain words and/or concepts from Topic B, the second analogy should contain words or concepts from Topic C, and the third analogy should contain words and/or concepts from Topic D. Make sure you suggest an answer AND establish a relationship sentence for each analogy.

Be prepared to place your analogies (without the answer or the relationship sentence) on the board as your instructor may direct and to lead your classmates in their attempt to solve your analogies. Also ask your classmates to determine from which Topic in this book your analogies came.

E4.   Here is another, more complex, form of the analogy, generally seen on many I.Q. and college entrance tests.

abstract : common :: _____ : _____

a. past tense : verb   c. verb : past tense
b. nominative : 1st person   d. singular : plural

As you can see, you must choose the second pair of words from the choices given. The process to solve this kind of analogy is different from the previous example.

THE PROCESS FOR SOLUTION

STEP ONE. Establish a tentative relationship between Word 1 and Word 2 and place it in the space above. In this case, *abstract* and *common* are both characteristics of a noun. So we can say that the relationship is *the first word and the second word are both characteristics of nouns.*

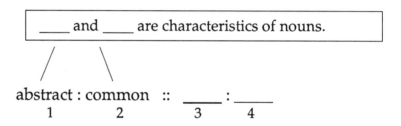

____ and ____ are characteristics of nouns.

abstract : common :: ____ : ____
    1   2   3   4

STEP TWO. Now you are ready to examine the four choices. Place the pair of words from each choice into the relationship sentence established for Word 1 and Word 2 and determine which of the four choices given can use that relationship sentence without change.

a.

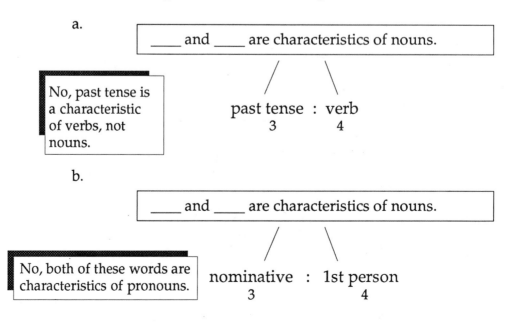

____ and ____ are characteristics of nouns.

No, past tense is a characteristic of verbs, not nouns.

past tense : verb
    3   4

b.

____ and ____ are characteristics of nouns.

No, both of these words are characteristics of pronouns.

nominative : 1st person
     3   4

c.

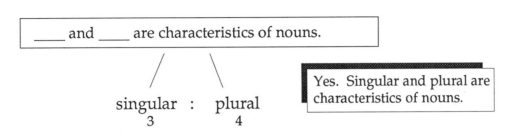

___ and ___ are characteristics of nouns.

verb : past tense
  3   4

No, verb and past tense are
not characteristics of nouns.

d.

___ and ___ are characteristics of nouns.

singular : plural
  3   4

Yes. Singular and plural are
characteristics of nouns.

STEP THREE.   Now, make a choice based on your evidence. The choice that
gives a relationship exactly like that of the original pair is the correct choice.

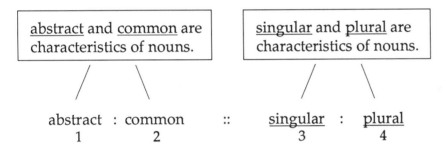

abstract and common are
characteristics of nouns.

singular and plural are
characteristics of nouns.

abstract : common   ::   singular : plural
    1   2   3   4

PRACTICE

E5.   Here are some analogies for you to do. Follow the steps outlined above
by: Writing (1) the terms you are comparing below the lines, (2) the
relationship sentence in the box, and (3) your conclusion for each set in the
margin. The process is just as important as the answer. Be prepared to
defend your answers in class.

APPLYING

1.   dark : adjective :: ___ : ___

    a. adjective : adverb   c. too : adverb
    b. adverb : adjective   d. light : adverb

STEP ONE.

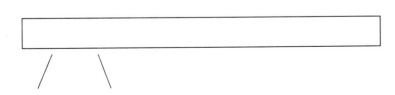

STEP TWO.

a.

b.

c.

d.

STEP THREE.

2.   I : They :: _____ : _____

   a. she : us   c. we : he
   b. me : them   d. you : her

STEP ONE.

STEP TWO.

a.

b.

```
┌─────────────────────────────────────────┐
│                                           │
└─────────────────────────────────────────┘
      /        \
```

c.

```
┌─────────────────────────────────────────┐
│                                           │
└─────────────────────────────────────────┘
      /        \
```

d.

```
┌─────────────────────────────────────────┐
│                                           │
└─────────────────────────────────────────┘
      /        \
```

STEP THREE.

```
┌──────────────────────┐      ┌──────────────────────┐
│                      │      │                      │
└──────────────────────┘      └──────────────────────┘
       /      \                      /      \
```

3.   noun : object of preposition:: ___ : ____

    a. noun : plural   c. verb : verb
    b. pronoun : pronoun   d. pronoun : direct object

STEP ONE.

```
┌─────────────────────────────────────────┐
│                                           │
└─────────────────────────────────────────┘
      /        \
```

STEP TWO.

a.

```
┌─────────────────────────────────────────┐
│                                           │
└─────────────────────────────────────────┘
      /        \
```

b.

```
┌─────────────────────────────────────────┐
│                                           │
└─────────────────────────────────────────┘
      /        \
```

c.

d.

STEP THREE.

4. cat : jumps :: _____ : _____

    a. boy : girl   c. hop : skip
    b. she : goes   d. dog : animal

STEP ONE.

STEP TWO.

a.

b.

c.

d.

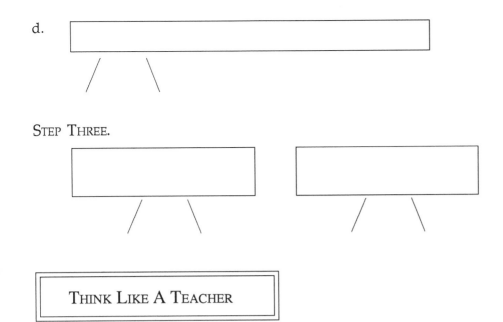

STEP THREE.

THINK LIKE A TEACHER

CREATING

E6. Now it's your turn to create some analogies. Develop six analogies in the same form as those presented in E5. Provide four choices only one of which will be correct. The first two analogies should contain words and/or concepts from Topic B, the third and fourth analogies should contain words or concepts from Topic C, and the fifth and sixth analogy should contain words and/or concepts from Topic D. Make sure you suggest an answer AND propose a relationship sentence for each analogy.

Be prepared to place your analogies and choices (without indicating the answer or the relationship sentence) on the board as your instructor may direct and to ask your classmates to solve your analogies.

A THIRD FORM OF ANALOGIES

PREDICTING

E7. Here is an analogy that leaves Word 1 and Word 4 blank. Detail the steps you would take to solve this kind of analogy. Don't forget you can't establish a relationship between Word 2 and Word 3; the relationship must be between Word 1 and Word 2, and then between Word 3 and Word 4.

$$\underset{1}{\underline{\quad\quad}} : \underset{2}{\text{infinitive}} :: \underset{3}{\text{him}} : \underset{4}{\underline{\quad\quad}}$$

a. gerund : her
b. to run : objective pron.
c. walked : objective pron.
d. to run : himself

E8.   Compare your strategy to the one proposed below.

STEP ONE.

In this kind of analogy, I cannot establish a single relationship sentence for the first set of words. So I will have to establish a pair of relationship sentences for each of the choices and determine which pair of choices uses the same relationship sentence.

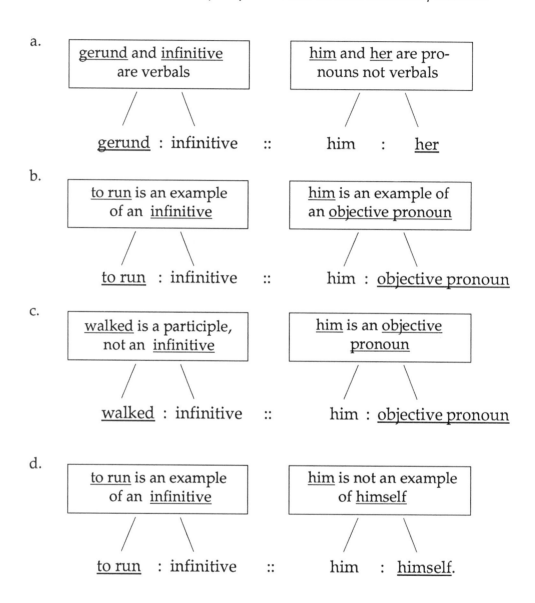

a.

> gerund and infinitive
> are verbals

gerund : infinitive   ::

> him and her are pro-
> nouns not verbals

him : her

b.

> to run is an example
> of an infinitive

to run : infinitive   ::

> him is an example of
> an objective pronoun

him : objective pronoun

c.

> walked is a participle,
> not an infinitive

walked : infinitive   ::

> him is an objective
> pronoun

him : objective pronoun

d.

> to run is an example
> of an infinitive

to run : infinitive   ::

> him is not an example
> of himself

him : himself.

STEP TWO.

I will choose b as the answer since the very same relationship sentence is used for both sets of words.

Which strategy (your own or the one suggested) did you determine you will use and why?

E9.   Using the strategy of your choice, solve the following analogy problems. Besides writing the relationship sentence and circling the correct
answer, be prepared to explain the reasons for rejecting the choices not
chosen.

APPLYING

1.
_____ : compound :: complex : _____

a. go : will have gone   c. verb : sentence
b. common : singular   d. simple : comp./complex

RELATIONSHIP SENTENCE:

2.
_____ : man :: go : _____

a. women : goes   c. singular : plural
b. goes : men   d. noun : verb

RELATIONSHIP SENTENCE:

3.
_____ : nominative :: him : _____

a. objective : he   c. objective : possessive
b. she : possessive   d. he : objective

RELATIONSHIP SENTENCE:

4.

_____ : subordinate :: main : _____

a. dependent : independent
b. clause : verb
c. dependent : verb
d. coordinate : helping

RELATIONSHIP SENTENCE:

5.

_____ : subject :: pronoun : _____

a. noun : subject
b. antecedent : reference
c. verb : antecedent
d. singular : agreement

RELATIONSHIP SENTENCE:

THINK LIKE A TEACHER

CREATING

E10. Now it's your turn to create some analogies. Develop six analogies in the same form as those presented in E9, with blank words on each end of the problem and four possible answers from which to choose. The first two analogies should contain words and/or concepts from Topic B, the next two analogies should contain words or concepts from Topic C, and the final two analogies should contain words and/or concepts from Topic D. Make sure you suggest an answer AND propose a relationship sentence for each analogy. Don't have the answer too obvious by making the wrong choices clearly incorrect.

Be prepared to place your analogies and choices (without indicating the answer or the relationship sentence) on the board as your instructor may direct for your classmates to solve.

EVALUATE PROCESS

E11. You have completed analogy exercises using grammatical terms. This is the first of a series of questions to help you evaluate the experience.

What have you learned about analogies?

E12. Did solving these analogies help you understand grammatical terms?

Why or why not?

E13. Did <u>creating</u> analogies help you understand grammatical terms?

Why or why not?

E14. Which is a better way to learn about analogies, solving analogies or creating analogies?

Why?

EVALUATING

E15. Which is a better way to learn grammatical terms, solving or creating analogies which use grammatical terms?

Why?

E16. Compare the mental process you go through to answer analogies created by someone else and the mental processes you went through to create your own analogies.

COMPARING

E17. By which process (answering others' analogies or creating your own) do you learn better and why?

E18. Discuss your answers to E11 through E17 with the class. Note here any insights that you want to remember from the class discussion.

DISCUSSING

E19. Write a four page composition on how you can use the techniques you experienced throughout this book to learn material in other classes. This paper will be graded partly on grammar. So develop an important strategy: How to proofread your own work for grammatical errors.

ANALYZE A SENTENCE: PARTS OF SPEECH, CHARACTERISTICS, AND FUNCTIONS

E20. This last exercise in analyzing a sentence starts out the same as the others. That is, you should label the part of speech, the characteristics, and the function of each word. In addition, however, note in the space around the boxes any and all comments you want to make about the the words, the sentence, the course, or anything else that comes to mind as you do the exercise. It is the final exercise for you TO BE AWARE OF YOUR THOUGHT PROCESS, the concept used in the very first Topic of this book.

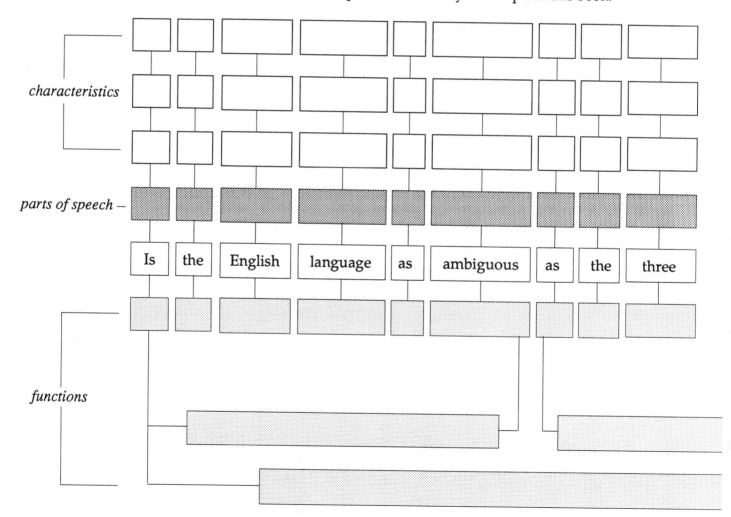

characteristics

parts of speech —

Is | the | English | language | as | ambiguous | as | the | three

functions

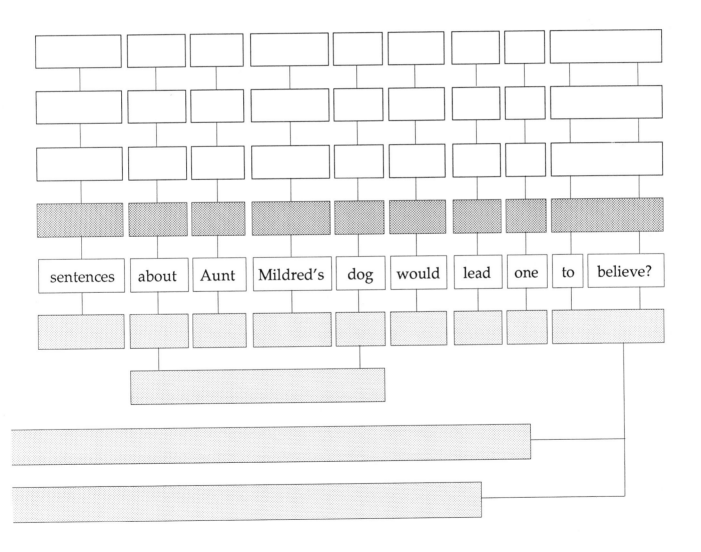

sentences | about | Aunt | Mildred's | dog | would | lead | one | to | believe?